favourite
easy meals

over 100 recipes to enjoy

First published in 2010
LOVE FOOD is an imprint of Parragon Books Ltd

Parragon
Queen Street House
4 Queen Street
Bath BA1 1HE, UK

ISBN 978-1-4075-4762-6

Printed in China

Cover design by Andrew Easton at Ummagumma
Photography by Günter Beer
Home economy by Stevan Paul
Additional photography for 'Snacks' by Clive Bozzard-Hill, Karen Thomas and Laurie Evans
Additional home economy for 'Snacks' by Stevan Paul, Sandra Baddeley, Sue Henderson, Valerie Berry, Annie Rigg and Phillippa Vanstone

Notes for the reader
This book uses both metric and imperial measurements. Follow the same units of measurement throughout; do not mix metric and imperial. All spoon measurements are level: teaspoons are assumed to be 5 ml, and tablespoons are assumed to be 15 ml. Unless otherwise stated, milk is assumed to be full fat, eggs and individual vegetables are medium, and pepper is freshly ground black pepper.

The times given are an approximate guide only. Preparation times differ according to the techniques used by different people and the cooking times may also vary from those given. Optional ingredients, variations or serving suggestions have not been included in the calculations.

Recipes using raw or very lightly cooked eggs should be avoided by infants, the elderly, pregnant women, convalescents and anyone suffering from an illness. Pregnant and breastfeeding women are advised to avoid eating peanuts and peanut products. Sufferers from nut allergies should be aware that some of the ready-made ingredients used in the recipes in this book may contain nuts. Always check the packaging before use.

Vegetarians should be aware that some of the ready-made ingredients used in the recipes in this book may contain animal products. Always check the packaging before use.

Contents

Introduction

If you think that the word 'easy' equates to the phrase 'mediocre and boring', prepare to eat your words. Better still, why not munch some irresistible snacks, scrumptious pizzas, luscious wraps, fabulous finger food and desserts to die for? About the only thing easier than preparing the terrific meals in this book is eating them.

Of course, there are times when only a hearty, slow-cooked casserole or a roast dinner with all the trimmings will fit the bill, but there are plenty of other occasions when no one wants to expend a lot of time and effort in the kitchen – a lovely summer's evening, an informal gathering of friends, Friday night at the end of a frantically busy week, Saturday lunchtime… This superb collection of well over 100 recipes is the answer, whether you want a light meal, a more substantial dish or just something a bit different.

Life is very demanding these days – make it easier by matching the meal to the mood and time with trouble-free dishes at your fingertips.

This book is divided into four sections and each section contains several chapters, making it simplicity itself to find exactly the easy meal that suits you and your family, whatever the occasion. Whether you want to curl up on the sofa with a plate of something tasty and satisfying while you watch your favourite soap, a quick lunch before going out to buy the week's groceries, a late-night treat when you've been to the movies, something to keep the kids going when you're all off to the match, a colourful mix-and-match tapas- or meze-style supper for family and friends or a special, but effortless, sweet indulgence to end a midweek family supper, you will be spoilt for choice. There are even some great accompaniments that will complement main course recipes, from the many easy dishes in this book to the routine steaks, chops and sausages that we all cook on a regular basis.

With recipes inspired by cuisines from around the world you are sure to find plenty of easy meals that are just right for you and your family, whatever your favourite flavours and ingredients – hot Thai treats and spicy Mexican wraps, refreshing Middle Eastern dips and salads and classic bite-sized Mediterranean delicacies, fruity desserts and mouth-watering crêpes, not to mention an impressive array of almost every pizza topping imaginable. Whether you're a beginner or an experienced cook, you're bound to make short work of all these and many more delights.

Easy extras

As well as the recipes for tasty rice and vegetable dishes, salads and dips that can double as sauces which you will find in this book, there are plenty of other side dishes and accompaniments for hassle-free meals. Mixed salad leaves go with almost everything and are available ready-washed in most supermarkets. All they require is a simple dressing. You can buy a variety of ready-made dressings or, more economically, simply whisk together 3 parts olive oil and 1 part wine vinegar or lemon juice and season with salt and pepper. If you feel like it, you can whisk in a little Dijon mustard and add some fresh herbs too. Raw vegetables, such as grated carrot, sliced onion, diced cucumber, celery sticks, spring onions and chopped tomatoes, can make a salad more interesting and attractive and are both healthy and nutritious. Grated cheese adds extra protein and flavour and if you're feeling really lazy, you can buy it already grated. You can also add a handful of mixed seeds or chopped nuts to produce a perfect side dish made in minutes.

It's worth keeping your store cupboard stocked with bottled and canned items that can be used as garnishes or added to salads. Capers, whole and stuffed olives, preserved baby artichokes, peppers, mushrooms and aubergines, pickled chillies and your favourite chutneys and sauces are all useful, time-saving additions that can turn your easy meal into an easy feast.

Nowadays, the choice of fresh bread and rolls in most supermarkets is huge and ranges from Middle Eastern flatbreads to Italian breadsticks and from sourdough to herbed and spiced loaves with or without cheese. They won't go with everything but are good with some dishes, providing healthy carbohydrate. Garlic bread – home-made or ready-made – is also a tasty and popular extra that only requires heating.

Almost instant sauces, based on ordinary or Greek-style yogurt, double cream, crème fraîche, soured cream or soft cheese can add the finishing touch to a meal. Just add snipped fresh chives or chopped fresh herbs, sliced spring onions, sun-dried tomato paste, tapenade (black olive and caper paste) or any type of ready-made pesto, then mix together until the blend suits your taste. You can also make easy salsas with tropical fruit, such as mango, papaya or pineapple, spring onions, fresh chillies or Tabasco sauce and lemon juice. Again, just mix together until you like the combination of flavours.

Snacks

Juggling duty and desire is part of the modern lifestyle, and the way we eat matches our kaleidoscope of commitments. Many people work away from home and each day is not necessarily identical to the last. There are frequent days when family members are busy with separate activities and need to eat at different times. It is therefore not always easy to plan for, prepare and eat formal meals. Eating small amounts frequently fits busy lifestyles – snatched breakfasts, mid-morning snacks, packed lunches, after-work snacks and late, but light, suppers are typical eating occasions.

Social snacking

From a casual buffet to a formal canapé party, festive gatherings are classic snacking occasions. When feeding a crowd, two or three home-made items will transform a basic selection of nuts, crisps, crackers and other bought snacks, making them more interesting and substantial.

Here are some tips to make entertaining easy:
• The best party snacks can be prepared ahead and cooked at the last minute with minimum fuss, or served cold.
• Fit the presentation to the occasion – snacks lined up on platters with stylish garnishes look impressive.
• Instead of plates, have bright paper napkins to wipe sticky fingers.
• Put out bowls where guests can deposit discarded cocktail sticks.
• Stagger snacks during a party, handing out alternating trays of different types.

Minimum effort: maximum flavour

Take-away food tends to be full of fat, misses out on good nutrients, and comes in portion sizes that make us eat more than we need. The TV Snacks chapter has recipes that are the right compromise for times

when slaving over a hot hob is not an option. Unlike their bought counterparts, these are free from artificial additives, and are fresh and delicious. Oven-fried Chicken Wings, Home-made Oven Fries, and Classic Spare Ribs need minimum attention once they're in the oven. Add a bag of prepared salad and follow on with some fresh fruit for a vitamin boost.

Light lunches or late nights

Lighter eating is good when working late, socializing in the early evening, or providing a cab service for children's out-of-school activities. It's often late evening before there's a chance to sit and eat, and satisfying but light dishes are best. Eating light occasionally is also good for keeping weight in check. Spicy Prawns, Parma Ham with Melon & Asparagus, or Red Cabbage Slaw are good examples of suitable dishes. Keep breads in the freezer, ready cut for thawing in the microwave – ciabatta, bagels, crusty French bread or close-textured

light rye make light dishes more substantial. Instant couscous can be ready in minutes to complement light dishes without making them too stodgy.

Eating out and about

Here are a few reminders for practical packed lunches:
• Use insulated containers and/or bags and drinks holders to keep food fresh. They come in all sizes, from individual pots to picnic hampers for a feast.
• For warming drinks or soups, small Thermos flasks are ideal. Insulated pots are good for chunky soups or stews.
• Fresh fruit and/or salad or raw vegetable sticks are vital in daily packed lunches. For salads on the go, make sure to pack dressings in a screw-top pot and add them at the last minute to keep salad leaves crisp.
• Try cook-ahead foods for a meal one day and packed lunch the next: make Spanish Omelette for supper, and chill some for a packed lunch. Soups and sushi can also be prepared ahead.

Mouth-watering Morsels

serves 4

3 skinless, boneless chicken breasts

4 tbsp wholemeal plain flour

1 tbsp wheatgerm

1/2 tsp ground cumin

1/2 tsp ground coriander

1 egg, lightly beaten

2 tbsp olive oil

pepper

green salad, to serve

for the dipping sauce

100 g/3$\frac{1}{2}$ oz sunblush tomatoes

100 g/3$\frac{1}{2}$ oz fresh tomatoes, peeled, deseeded and chopped

2 tbsp mayonnaise

chicken nuggets

Preheat the oven to 190°C/375°F/Gas Mark 5. Cut the chicken breasts into 4-cm/1$\frac{1}{2}$-inch chunks. Mix the flour, wheatgerm, cumin, coriander, and pepper to taste in a bowl, then divide in half and put on 2 separate plates. Put the beaten egg on a third plate.

Pour the oil into a baking tray and heat in the oven. Roll the chicken pieces in one plate of flour, shake to remove any excess, then roll in the egg and in the second plate of flour, again shaking off any excess flour. When all the nuggets are ready, remove the baking tray from the oven and toss the nuggets in the hot oil. Roast in the oven for 25–30 minutes until golden and crisp.

Meanwhile, to make the dipping sauce, put both kinds of tomatoes in a blender or food processor and process until smooth. Add the mayonnaise and process again until well combined.

Remove the nuggets from the oven and drain on kitchen paper. Serve with the dipping sauce and a green salad.

serves 4

115 g/4 oz sirloin or rump
steak

4 button mushrooms,
cut into 1-cm/$1/2$-inch cubes

$1/2$ small onion, cut into
1-cm/$1/2$-inch cubes

*for the spicy tomato
marinade*

50 ml/2 fl oz tomato juice

50 ml/2 fl oz beef stock

1 tbsp Worcestershire sauce

1 tbsp lemon juice

2 tbsp dry sherry

few drops of Tabasco sauce

2 tbsp vegetable oil

1 tbsp minced celery

miniature beef kebabs

Cut the steak into 1-cm/$1/2$-inch cubes. Combine all the
marinade ingredients in a large, non-metallic bowl, whisk well
and stir in the meat, mushrooms and onion. Cover the bowl
with clingfilm and place in the refrigerator to marinate for
30 minutes.

Drain off the marinade. Place alternating pieces of steak and
vegetables on cocktail sticks, taking care not to pack them
together too tightly.

Preheat a griddle or heavy-based frying pan over a high heat.
Place the kebabs in the pan and cook, turning frequently, for
5 minutes, or until gently browned and cooked through.

Pile the kebabs high on platters and serve immediately.

serves 4

450 g/1 lb lean, finely minced lamb

1 medium onion

1 garlic clove, crushed

25 g/1 oz fresh white or brown breadcrumbs

1 tbsp chopped fresh mint

1 tbsp chopped fresh parsley

1 egg, beaten

olive oil, for brushing

salt and pepper

warm pitta bread and salad, to serve

grecian meatballs

Put the minced lamb in a bowl. Grate in the onion, then add the garlic, breadcrumbs, mint and parsley. Season well with salt and pepper. Mix the ingredients well then add the beaten egg and mix to bind the mixture together. Alternatively, the ingredients can be combined in the food processor.

With damp hands, form the mixture into 16 small balls and thread onto 4 flat metal skewers. Lightly oil a grill pan and brush the meatballs with oil.

Preheat the grill and cook the meatballs under a medium heat for 10 minutes, turning frequently, and brushing with more oil if necessary, until browned. Serve the meatballs tucked into warm pitta bread with salad.

serves 2

2 large white fish fillets, such
as sole, skinned

1 egg, beaten

3 heaped tbsp plain flour

vegetable oil, for deep-frying

lemon wedges, to garnish

for the garlic mayonnaise

6 tbsp mayonnaise

2 garlic cloves, crushed

fish goujons with garlic mayonnaise

Combine the mayonnaise and garlic in a small dish. Cover with clingfilm and refrigerate while you cook the fish.

Cut the fish into 2.5-cm/1-inch strips. Dip the strips in the egg, then drain and dredge in flour.

Meanwhile, heat the oil in a deep-fryer or large saucepan to 180–190°C/350–375°F, or until a cube of bread browns in 30 seconds. Fry the pieces of fish in the hot oil for 3–4 minutes, or until golden brown. Remove from the oil and drain on kitchen paper.

Remove the garlic mayonnaise from the refrigerator and stir once. Serve the fish goujons in a bowl, garnished with lemon wedges, with the mayonnaise on the side for dipping.

makes 20

200 g/7 oz canned tuna in
spring water, drained

1 egg, beaten

1 tsp finely chopped
fresh parsley

50 g/1¾ oz fresh wholemeal
breadcrumbs

about 1 tbsp wholemeal
plain flour

vegetable oil, for brushing

salt and pepper

tuna bites

Mash the tuna with the egg, parsley, and a pinch of salt and
pepper to taste. Add the breadcrumbs and mix well, then add
enough of the flour to bind the mixture together.

Divide the mixture into 20 mini portions, shape each portion
into a ball and chill for 15 minutes.

Meanwhile, preheat the oven to 190°C/375°F/Gas Mark 5. Brush a
non-stick baking sheet with a little oil. Space the tuna balls out
on the baking sheet and brush with a little more oil. Bake in the
preheated oven for 15–20 minutes until golden and crisp.

Remove from the oven and drain on kitchen paper. Serve warm
or cold.

serves 4

225 g/8 oz dried chickpeas

1 large onion, finely chopped

1 garlic clove, crushed

2 tbsp chopped fresh parsley,
plus extra sprigs to garnish

2 tsp ground cumin

2 tsp ground coriander

1/2 tsp baking powder

cayenne pepper

oil, for deep-frying

salt

to serve

hummus (see page 314)

tomato wedges

pitta bread

falafel

Soak the chickpeas overnight in enough cold water to cover
them and allow room for expansion. Drain, then place in a
saucepan, cover with fresh water and bring to the boil. Reduce
the heat and simmer for 1 hour, or until tender. Drain.

Place the chickpeas in a food processor and blend to make a
coarse paste. Add the onion, garlic, parsley, cumin, coriander,
baking powder, and cayenne pepper and salt to taste. Blend
again to mix thoroughly.

Cover and leave to rest for 30 minutes, then shape into 8 balls.
Leave to rest for a further 30 minutes. Heat the oil in a wok or
large saucepan to 180–190°C/350–375°F, or until a cube of bread
browns in 30 seconds. Gently drop in the balls and cook until
golden brown. Remove from the oil and drain on kitchen paper.

Serve hot or at room temperature with hummus, tomato wedges
and pitta bread. Garnish with sprigs of parsley.

serves 4

115 g/4 oz fresh white bread

2 tbsp freshly grated
Parmesan cheese

1 tsp paprika

2 egg whites

225 g/8 oz button
mushrooms

for the aïoli

4 garlic cloves, crushed

2 egg yolks

225 ml/8 fl oz extra virgin
olive oil

salt and pepper

mushroom bites with aïoli

Preheat the oven to 190°C/375°F/Gas Mark 5. To make the aïoli, put the garlic in a bowl, add a pinch of salt and mash with the back of a spoon. Add the egg yolks and beat with an electric whisk for 30 seconds, or until creamy. Start beating in the oil, one drop at a time. As the mixture begins to thicken, add the oil in a steady stream, beating constantly. Season to taste with salt and pepper, cover the bowl with clingfilm and chill in the refrigerator until required.

Line a large baking sheet with baking paper. Grate the bread into breadcrumbs and place them in a bowl with the Parmesan cheese and paprika. Lightly whisk the egg whites in a separate clean bowl, then dip each mushroom first into the egg whites, then into the breadcrumbs, and place on the prepared baking sheet.

Bake in the preheated oven for 15 minutes, or until the coating is crisp and golden. Serve immediately with the aïoli.

serves 4

sunflower oil, for
deep-frying

1 large egg

pinch of salt

175 ml/6 fl oz water

55 g/2 oz plain flour

2 tsp ground cinnamon

55 g/2 oz caster sugar

4 eating apples, peeled
and cored

apple fritters

Pour the sunflower oil into a deep fryer or large, heavy-based saucepan and heat to 180–190°C/350–375°F, or until a cube of bread browns in 30 seconds.

Mix together the egg and salt until frothy, then quickly whisk in the water and flour. Do not overbeat the batter – it doesn't matter if it isn't completely smooth.

Mix together the cinnamon and sugar in a shallow dish and reserve.

Slice the apples into 5-mm/¼-inch-thick rings. Spear with a fork, 1 slice at a time, and dip in the batter to coat. Add to the hot oil, in batches, and cook for 1 minute on each side, or until golden and puffed up. Remove with a slotted spoon and drain on kitchen paper. Keep warm while you cook the remaining batches. Transfer to a large serving plate, sprinkle with the cinnamon sugar and serve.

serves 6

600 ml/1 pint good-quality
ice cream

200 g/7 oz plain chocolate

2 tbsp unsalted butter

chocolate ice-cream bites

Line a baking tray with clingfilm.

Using a melon baller, scoop out balls of ice cream and place them on the prepared baking tray. Alternatively, cut the ice cream into bite-size cubes. Stick a cocktail stick in each piece and return to the freezer until very hard.

Place the chocolate and the butter in a heatproof bowl set over a saucepan of gently simmering water until melted. Quickly dip the frozen ice-cream balls into the warm chocolate and return to the freezer. Keep them there until ready to serve.

2

TV Snacks

serves 4

900 g/2 lb pork spare ribs

coriander sprigs, to garnish

for the marinade

2 tbsp dark soy sauce

3 tbsp hoisin sauce

1 tbsp Chinese rice wine or
dry sherry

pinch of Chinese five
spice powder

2 tsp dark brown sugar

1/4 tsp chilli sauce

2 garlic cloves, crushed

classic spare ribs

Cut the spare ribs into separate pieces if they are joined
together. If desired, you can chop them into 5-cm/2-inch lengths,
using a cleaver.

Mix together the soy sauce, hoisin sauce, Chinese rice wine,
Chinese five spice powder, dark brown sugar, chilli sauce and
garlic in a large bowl.

Place the ribs in a shallow dish and pour the mixture over them,
turning to coat them well. Cover and marinate in the refrigerator,
turning the ribs from time to time, for at least 1 hour.

Remove the ribs from the marinade and arrange them in a single
layer on a wire rack placed over a roasting tin half-filled with
warm water. Brush with the marinade, reserving the remainder.

Cook in a preheated oven, at 180°C/350°F/Gas Mark 4, for
30 minutes. Remove the roasting tin from the oven and turn the
ribs over. Brush with the remaining marinade and return to the
oven for a further 30 minutes, or until cooked through. Transfer
to a warmed serving dish, garnish with the coriander sprigs and
serve immediately.

serves 4

2 tbsp vegetable or groundnut oil

1 tbsp sesame oil

juice of 1/2 lime

2 skinless, boneless chicken breasts, cut into small cubes

for the dip

2 tbsp vegetable or groundnut oil

1 small onion, finely chopped

1 small fresh green chilli, deseeded and chopped

1 garlic clove, finely chopped

125 ml/4 fl oz crunchy peanut butter

6–8 tbsp water

juice of 1/2 lime

crushed peanuts, to garnish

chicken satay

Combine both the oils and the lime juice in a non-metallic dish. Add the chicken cubes, cover with clingfilm and chill for 1 hour.

To make the dip, heat the oil in a frying pan and fry the onion, chilli and garlic over a low heat, stirring occasionally, for about 5 minutes, until just softened. Add the peanut butter, water and lime juice and simmer gently, stirring constantly, until the peanut butter has softened enough to make a dip – you may need to add extra water to make a thinner consistency.

Meanwhile, drain the chicken cubes and thread them onto 8–12 presoaked wooden skewers. Put under a hot grill or on a barbecue, turning frequently, for about 10 minutes, until cooked and browned. Serve hot with the warm dip, garnished with crushed peanuts.

serves 4

12 chicken wings

1 egg

50 ml/2 fl oz milk

4 heaped tbsp plain flour

1 tsp paprika

225 g/8 oz breadcrumbs

55 g/2 oz butter

salt and pepper

oven-fried chicken wings

Preheat the oven to 220°C/425°F/Gas Mark 7. Separate the chicken wings into 3 pieces each. Discard the bony tip. Beat the egg with the milk in a shallow dish. Combine the flour, paprika and salt and pepper to taste in a separate shallow dish. Place the breadcrumbs in another shallow dish.

Dip the chicken pieces into the egg to coat well, then drain and roll in the seasoned flour. Remove, shaking off any excess, and roll the chicken in the breadcrumbs, gently pressing them onto the surface, then shaking off any excess.

Melt the butter in the preheated oven in a shallow roasting tin large enough to hold all the chicken pieces in a single layer. Arrange the chicken, skin-side down, in the tin and bake in the oven for 10 minutes. Turn and bake for a further 10 minutes, or until the chicken is tender and the juices run clear when a skewer is inserted into the thickest part of the meat.

Remove the chicken from the tin and arrange on a large platter. Serve hot or at room temperature.

serves 6

400 g/14 oz canned
white crabmeat

1–2 fresh bird's eye
chillies, to taste, deseeded
and finely chopped

6 spring onions,
finely shredded

1 courgette, grated

1 carrot, grated

1 small yellow pepper,
deseeded and finely
shredded

85 g/3 oz fresh beansprouts,
rinsed

1 tbsp chopped fresh
coriander

1 large egg white

1–2 tbsp sunflower oil

for the salsa

1 bird's eye chilli, deseeded
and finely chopped

5-cm/2-inch piece
cucumber, grated

1 tbsp chopped fresh
coriander

1 tbsp lime juice

1 tbsp Thai sweet chilli sauce

1 tbsp peanuts, finely
chopped (optional)

thai-style fishcakes

Mix together all the fishcake ingredients, except for the egg white and oil. Whisk the egg white until frothy and just beginning to stiffen then stir into the crab mixture. Then, using your hands, press about 1–2 tablespoons of the mixture together to form a fishcake. Repeat until 12 fishcakes are formed.

To make the salsa, combine all the ingredients except for the peanuts. Spoon into a small bowl, cover and leave for 30 minutes for the flavours to develop. Sprinkle with the peanuts, if using.

Heat 1 teaspoon of the oil in a non-stick frying pan over a low heat. Cook the fishcakes over a medium heat in batches for 2 minutes on each side until lightly browned. Take care when turning them over. Remove and drain on kitchen paper. Repeat until all the fishcakes are cooked, using more oil if necessary. Serve immediately with the salsa.

serves 6

175 g/6 oz tortilla chips

400 g/14 oz canned refried beans, warmed

2 tbsp finely chopped bottled jalapeño chillies

200 g/7 oz canned or bottled pimentos or roasted peppers, drained and finely sliced

115 g/4 oz Gruyère cheese, grated

115 g/4 oz Cheddar cheese, grated

salt and pepper

nachos

Preheat the oven to 200°C/400°F/Gas Mark 6.

Spread the tortilla chips out over the base of a large, shallow, ovenproof dish or roasting tin. Cover with the warmed refried beans. Scatter over the chillies and pimentos and season to taste with salt and pepper. Mix together the cheeses in a bowl and sprinkle on top.

Bake in the preheated oven for 5–8 minutes, or until the cheese is bubbling and melted. Serve immediately.

serves 4

150 g/5½ oz long-grain rice

3 eggs, beaten

2 tbsp vegetable oil

2 garlic cloves, crushed

4 spring onions, chopped

125 g/4½ oz cooked peas

1 tbsp light soy sauce

pinch of salt

shredded spring onion,
to garnish

egg fried rice

Cook the rice in a pan of boiling water for 10–12 minutes, until almost cooked, but not soft. Drain well, rinse under cold water and drain again.

Place the beaten eggs in a non-stick saucepan and cook over a gentle heat, stirring until softly scrambled.

Heat the vegetable oil in a preheated wok or large frying pan, swirling the oil around the base of the wok until it is really hot.

Add the crushed garlic, spring onions and peas and sauté, stirring occasionally, for 1–2 minutes. Stir the rice into the wok, mixing to combine.

Add the eggs, light soy sauce and a pinch of salt to the wok or frying pan and stir to mix in the egg thoroughly.

Transfer the egg fried rice to serving dishes and serve garnished with the shredded spring onion.

serves 4

4 x 225 g/8 oz baking
potatoes

2 tsp olive oil

coarse sea salt and pepper

for the guacamole dip

175 g/6 oz ripe avocado

1 tbsp lemon juice

2 ripe, firm tomatoes,
finely chopped

1 tsp grated lemon rind

100 g/3$1/2$ oz low-fat soft cheese
with herbs and garlic

4 spring onions,
finely chopped

a few drops of Tabasco sauce

salt and pepper, to taste

potato skins with guacamole

Bake the potatoes in a preheated oven at 200°C/400°F/Gas Mark 6 for 1$1/4$ hours. Remove from the oven and allow to cool for 30 minutes. Reset the oven to 220°C/425°F/Gas Mark 7.

Halve the potatoes lengthways and scoop out 2 tablespoons of the flesh. Place the skins on a baking sheet and brush the flesh side lightly with oil. Sprinkle with salt and pepper. Bake for a further 25 minutes until golden and crisp.

To make the guacamole dip, mash the avocado with the lemon juice. Add the remaining ingredients and mix. Transfer to a serving bowl.

Drain the potato skins on paper towels and transfer to a warmed serving platter. Serve hot with the guacamole dip.

serves 4

450 g/1 lb potatoes, peeled

2 tbsp sunflower oil

salt and pepper

ketchup and mayonnaise,
to serve (optional)

home-made oven fries

Preheat the oven to 200°C/400°F/Gas Mark 6.

Cut the potatoes into thick, even-sized chips. Rinse them under cold running water, then dry well on a clean tea towel. Put in a bowl, add the oil and toss together until thoroughly coated.

Spread the chips on a baking sheet and cook in the preheated oven for 40–45 minutes, turning once, until golden. Add salt and pepper to taste and serve hot with ketchup and mayonnaise, if desired.

makes about 250 g/9 oz

3 tbsp sunflower oil

70 g/2^{1}/$_{2}$ oz popcorn

25 g/1 oz butter

55 g/2 oz light soft brown sugar

2 tbsp golden syrup

1 tbsp milk

55 g/2 oz plain chocolate chips

chocolate popcorn

Preheat the oven to 150°C/300°F/Gas Mark 2. Heat the oil in a large, heavy-based saucepan. Add the popcorn, cover the saucepan, and cook, vigorously and frequently shaking the saucepan, for about 2 minutes, until the popping stops. Turn into a large bowl.

Put the butter, sugar, golden syrup and milk in a saucepan and heat gently until the butter has melted. Bring to the boil, without stirring, and boil for 2 minutes. Remove from the heat, add the chocolate chips, and stir until melted.

Pour the chocolate mixture over the popcorn and toss together until evenly coated. Spread the mixture onto a large baking tray.

Bake the popcorn in the oven for about 15 minutes, until crisp. Leave to cool before serving.

Lighter Bites

serves 4

4 fillet steaks, about 115 g/
4 oz each, fat discarded

2 tbsp red wine vinegar

2 tbsp orange juice

2 tsp ready-made English
mustard

2 eggs

175 g/6 oz baby new potatoes

115 g/4 oz French beans,
trimmed

175 g/6 oz mixed salad
leaves, such as baby spinach,
rocket and mizuna

1 yellow pepper, peeled,
skinned and cut into strips

175 g/6 oz cherry tomatoes,
halved

black olives, stoned (optional)

2 tsp extra virgin olive oil

pepper

warm beef niçoise

Place the steaks in a shallow dish. Blend the vinegar with
1 tablespoon of the orange juice and 1 teaspoon of the mustard.
Pour over the steaks, cover and leave in the refrigerator for at least
30 minutes. Turn over halfway through the marinating time.

Place the eggs in a pan and cover with cold water. Bring to the
boil, then reduce the heat to a simmer and cook for 10 minutes.
Remove and plunge the eggs into cold water. Once cold, peel
and reserve.

Meanwhile, place the potatoes in a saucepan and cover with
cold water. Bring to the boil, cover and simmer for 15 minutes, or
until tender when pierced with a fork. Drain and reserve.

Bring a saucepan of water to the boil. Add the beans, cover and
simmer for 5–8 minutes, or until tender. Drain, plunge into cold
water then drain again and reserve. Meanwhile, arrange the
potatoes and beans on top of the salad leaves together with the
yellow pepper, cherry tomatoes and olives, if using. Chop the
hard-boiled eggs into wedges and add to the salad. Blend the
remaining orange juice and mustard with the olive oil, season to
taste with pepper and reserve.

Heat a griddle pan until smoking. Drain the steaks and cook for
3–5 minutes on each side or according to personal preference.
Slice the steaks and arrange on top of the salad, then pour over
the dressing and serve.

serves 4

225 g/8 oz baby asparagus spears

1 small or 1/2 medium-sized Galia or Canteloupe melon

55 g/2 oz Parma ham, thinly sliced

150 g/5 1/2 oz bag of mixed salad leaves, such as herb salad with rocket

85 g/3 oz fresh raspberries

1 tbsp freshly shaved Parmesan cheese

1 tbsp balsamic vinegar

2 tbsp raspberry vinegar

2 tbsp orange juice

parma ham with melon & asparagus

Trim the asparagus, cutting in half if very long. Cook in lightly boiled water over a medium heat for 5 minutes, or until tender. Drain and plunge into cold water then drain again and reserve.

Cut the melon in half and scoop out the seeds. Cut into small wedges and cut away the rind. Separate the Parma ham, cut the slices in half and wrap around the melon wedges.

Arrange the salad leaves on a large serving platter and place the melon wedges on top together with the asparagus spears.

Scatter over the raspberries and Parmesan shavings. Place the vinegars and orange juice in a screw-top jar and shake until blended. Pour over the salad and serve.

serves 4

4 skinless, boneless chicken
breasts, about 140 g/5 oz each

4 tsp Cajun seasoning

2 tsp sunflower oil

1 ripe mango, peeled, stoned
and cut into thick slices

200 g/7 oz mixed salad leaves

1 red onion, thinly sliced
and cut in half

175 g/6 oz cooked beetroot,
diced

85 g/3 oz radishes, sliced

55 g/2 oz walnut halves

4 tbsp walnut oil

1–2 tsp Dijon mustard

1 tbsp lemon juice

2 tbsp sesame seeds

salt and pepper

cajun chicken salad

Make 3 diagonal slashes across each chicken breast. Put the
chicken into a shallow dish and sprinkle all over with the Cajun
seasoning. Cover and refrigerate for at least 30 minutes.

When ready to cook, brush a griddle pan with the sunflower oil.
Heat over a high heat until very hot and a few drops of water
sprinkled into the pan sizzle immediately. Add the chicken and
cook for 7–8 minutes on each side, or until thoroughly cooked. If
still slightly pink in the centre, cook a little longer. Remove the
chicken and reserve.

Add the mango slices to the pan and cook for 2 minutes on each
side. Remove and reserve.

Meanwhile, arrange the salad leaves in a salad bowl and scatter
over the onion, beetroot, radishes and walnut halves.

Put the walnut oil, mustard, lemon juice, and salt and pepper to
taste in a screw-top jar and shake until well blended. Pour over
the salad and sprinkle with the sesame seeds.

Add the mango and chicken to the salad bowl and serve
immediately.

serves 4

115 g/4 oz cherry or baby plum tomatoes

several lettuce leaves

4 ripe tomatoes, roughly chopped

100 g/3¹/₂ oz smoked salmon

200 g/7 oz large cooked prawns, thawed if frozen

few fresh dill sprigs

pepper

warmed rolls or ciabatta bread, to serve

for the dressing

1 tbsp Dijon mustard

2 tsp caster sugar

2 tsp red wine vinegar

2 tbsp medium olive oil

tomato, salmon & prawn salad

Halve most of the cherry tomatoes. Place the lettuce leaves around the edge of a shallow bowl and add all the tomatoes and cherry tomatoes. Using scissors, snip the smoked salmon into strips and scatter over the tomatoes, then add the prawns.

Mix the mustard, sugar, vinegar and oil together in a small bowl, then tear most of the dill sprigs into it. Mix well and pour over the salad. Toss well to coat the salad with the dressing. Snip the remaining dill over the top and season to taste with pepper.

Serve the salad with warmed rolls or ciabatta bread.

serves 4

24 raw tiger prawns, thawed
if frozen

1 bay leaf

2 tbsp lime juice

1 tsp hot paprika

2 shallots, coarsely chopped

1 garlic clove, coarsely
chopped

1 tbsp light soy sauce

1 tbsp peanuts

1 tbsp desiccated coconut

1/2 red pepper, deseeded and
chopped

200 g/7 oz canned tomatoes

sunflower oil, for brushing

salt and pepper

lime wedges, to garnish

spicy prawns

Pull the heads off the prawns and peel off the shells. Place the heads, shells and bay leaf in a saucepan and add enough cold water to cover. Bring to the boil, then lower the heat and simmer for 30 minutes.

Meanwhile, using a sharp knife, cut along the back of each prawn. Remove the dark vein with the point of the knife. Place the prawns in a non-metallic dish and sprinkle with the lime juice and paprika. Season with salt and pepper and toss well to coat. Cover with clingfilm and leave to marinate in the refrigerator.

Put the shallots, garlic, soy sauce, peanuts, coconut and red pepper in a food processor. Drain the tomatoes, reserving 5 tablespoons of the can juice. Add the tomatoes and the reserved can juice to the food processor. Process until smooth. Scrape the mixture into a saucepan.

When the shellfish stock is ready, strain it into a measuring jug, pour it into the saucepan and bring the mixture to the boil, stirring occasionally. Lower the heat and simmer for 25–30 minutes until thickened.

Brush a griddle with oil and preheat. Remove the prawns from the refrigerator and thread them loosely onto skewers to make handling them easier. When the griddle is hot, add the prawns and cook for 2 minutes, or until they have changed colour and are cooked through.

Transfer the prawns to a serving dish – with or without the skewers – and garnish with lime wedges. Pour the dipping sauce into a bowl and serve with the prawns.

serves 4

280 g/10 oz buffalo
mozzarella, thinly sliced

8 tomatoes, sliced

20 fresh basil leaves

125 ml/4 fl oz extra virgin
olive oil

salt and pepper

three-colour salad

Arrange the mozzarella and tomato slices on 4 individual
serving plates and season to taste with salt. Set aside in a cool
place for 30 minutes.

Sprinkle the basil leaves over the salad and drizzle with the olive
oil. Season with pepper and serve immediately.

serves 6

450 g/1 lb red cabbage

1 eating apple

4 tbsp orange juice

1 large carrot, peeled and grated

1 red onion, peeled and cut into tiny wedges

175 g/6 oz cherry tomatoes, halved

7.5-cm/3-inch piece cucumber, peeled if preferred, and diced

55 g/2 oz fresh dates, stoned and chopped

1 tbsp extra virgin olive oil

1 tbsp chopped fresh flat-leaf parsley

pepper

red cabbage slaw

Discard the outer leaves and hard central core from the cabbage and shred finely. Wash thoroughly in plenty of cold water then shake dry and place in a salad bowl.

Core the apple and chop, toss in 1 tablespoon of the orange juice, then add to the salad bowl together with the carrot, onion, tomatoes, cucumber and dates.

Place the remaining orange juice in a screw-top jar, add the oil, parsley and pepper and shake until blended. Pour the dressing over the salad, toss lightly and serve.

serves 4–6

225–300 g/8–10$^{1}/_{2}$ oz mixed soft fruits, such as blueberries, raspberries and stoned fresh cherries

1$^{1}/_{2}$–2 tbsp Cointreau or orange flower water

250 g/9 oz mascarpone cheese

200 ml/7 fl oz crème fraîche

2–3 tbsp dark muscovado sugar

cheat's crème brûlée

Prepare the fruit, if necessary, and lightly rinse, then place in the bases of 4–6 x 150 ml/5 fl oz ramekin dishes. Sprinkle the fruit with the Cointreau.

Cream the mascarpone cheese in a bowl until soft, then gradually beat in the crème fraîche.

Spoon the cheese mixture over the fruit, smoothing the surface and ensuring that the tops are level. Chill in the refrigerator for at least 2 hours.

Sprinkle the tops with the sugar. Using a chef's blow torch, grill the tops until caramelized (about 2–3 minutes). Alternatively, cook under a preheated grill, turning the dishes, for 3–4 minutes, or until the tops are lightly caramelized all over.

Serve immediately or chill in the refrigerator for 15–20 minutes before serving.

makes 4

a selection of fruit,
such as apricots, peaches,
figs, strawberries, mangoes,
pineapple, bananas, dates
and pawpaw, prepared and
cut into chunks

maple syrup

50 g/1¾ oz plain chocolate
(minimum 70% cocoa solids),
broken into chunks

fruit skewers

Soak 4 bamboo skewers in water for at least 20 minutes.

Preheat the grill to high and line the grill pan with foil. Thread
alternate pieces of fruit onto each skewer. Brush the fruit with
a little maple syrup.

Put the chocolate in a heatproof bowl, set the bowl over a
saucepan of barely simmering water and heat until it is melted.

Meanwhile, cook the skewers under the preheated grill for
3 minutes, or until caramelized. Serve drizzled with a little
of the melted chocolate.

Food on the Go

serves 4–6

400g/14 oz can refried beans

8 flour tortillas

200 g/7 oz Cheddar cheese, grated

1 onion, chopped

1/2 bunch fresh coriander leaves, chopped, plus extra leaves to garnish

for the tomato salsa

6–8 ripe tomatoes, finely chopped

about 100 ml/3 1/2 fl oz tomato juice

3–4 garlic cloves, finely chopped

1/2 bunch fresh coriander leaves, coarsely chopped

pinch of sugar

3–4 fresh green chillies, deseeded and finely chopped

1/2–1 tsp ground cumin

3–4 spring onions, finely chopped

salt

cheese & bean quesadillas

Mix together all the ingredients in a bowl and season with salt to taste. Cover with clingfilm and chill in the refrigerator until required.

Place the beans in a small pan and set over a low heat to warm through.

Meanwhile, make the tortillas pliable by warming them gently in a lightly greased non-stick frying pan.

Remove the tortillas from the pan and quickly spread with a layer of warm beans. Top each tortilla with grated cheese, onion, fresh coriander and a spoonful of salsa. Roll up tightly.

Just before serving, heat the non-stick frying pan over a medium heat, sprinkling lightly with a couple of drops of water. Add the tortilla rolls, cover the pan and heat through until the cheese melts. Allow to brown lightly, if wished.

Remove the tortilla rolls from the pan and slice each roll, on the diagonal, into about 4 bite-size pieces. Serve the quesadillas hot or cold, garnished with coriander leaves.

serves 4

4 ciabatta rolls

2 tbsp olive oil

1 garlic clove, crushed

for the filling

1 red pepper

1 green pepper

1 yellow pepper

4 radishes, sliced

1 bunch of watercress

115 g/4 oz cream cheese

ciabatta rolls

Slice the ciabatta rolls in half. Heat the olive oil and garlic in a saucepan. Brush the garlic and oil mixture over the cut surfaces of the rolls and set aside.

Halve and deseed the peppers and place, skin-side up, on a grill rack. Cook under a preheated hot grill for 8–10 minutes until just beginning to char. Remove the peppers from the grill and place in a polythene bag. When cool enough to handle, peel and thinly slice.

Arrange the radish slices on 1 half of each roll with a few watercress leaves. Spoon the cream cheese on top. Pile the roasted peppers on top of the cream cheese and top with the other half of the roll. Serve immediately.

serves 4

140 g/5 oz butter

1 onion, finely chopped

1 garlic clove, finely chopped

250 g/9 oz chicken livers

1/2 tsp Dijon mustard

2 tbsp brandy (optional)

salt and pepper

brown toast fingers, to serve

for the clarified butter
(optional)

115 g/4 oz lightly salted
butter

chicken liver pâté

Melt half the butter in a large frying pan over a medium heat
and cook the onion for 3–4 minutes until soft and transparent.
Add the garlic and continue to cook for a further 2 minutes.

Check the chicken livers and remove any discoloured parts using
a pair of scissors. Add the livers to the frying pan and cook over
quite a high heat for 5–6 minutes until they are brown in colour.

Season well with salt and pepper and add the mustard and
brandy, if using.

Process the pâté in a blender or food processor until smooth.
Add the remaining butter cut into small pieces and process
again until creamy.

Press the pâté into a serving dish or 4 small ramekins, smooth
over the surface and cover with clingfilm. If the pâté is to be
kept for more than 2 days, you could cover the surface with a
little clarified butter. In a clean saucepan, heat the butter until
it melts, then continue heating for a few moments until it stops
bubbling. Allow the sediment to settle and carefully pour the
clarified butter over the pâté.

Chill in the refrigerator until ready to serve, then serve
accompanied by toast fingers.

serves 4

225 g/8 oz dried conchiglie (pasta shells)

50 g/1³/₄ oz pine kernels

350 g/12 oz cherry tomatoes, halved

1 red pepper, deseeded and cut into bite-sized chunks

1 red onion, chopped

200 g/7 oz buffalo mozzarella, cut into small pieces

12 black olives, stoned

25 g/1 oz fresh basil leaves

shavings of fresh Parmesan cheese, to garnish

crusty bread, to serve

for the dressing

5 tbsp extra virgin olive oil

2 tbsp balsamic vinegar

1 tbsp chopped fresh basil

salt and pepper

italian salad

Bring a large saucepan of lightly salted water to the boil. Add the pasta and cook over a medium heat for about 10 minutes, or according to the packet instructions. When cooked, the pasta should be tender but still firm to the bite. Drain, rinse under cold running water and drain again. Leave to cool.

While the pasta is cooking, put the pine kernels in a dry frying pan and cook over a low heat for 1–2 minutes until golden brown. Remove from the heat, transfer to a dish and leave to cool.

To make the dressing, put the oil, vinegar and basil into a small bowl. Season with salt and pepper and stir together well. Cover with clingfilm and set to one side.

To assemble the salad, divide the pasta between serving bowls. Add the pine kernels, tomatoes, red pepper, onion, cheese and olives. Scatter over the basil leaves, then drizzle over the dressing. Garnish with fresh Parmesan cheese shavings and serve with crusty bread.

serves 6

200 g/7 oz new potatoes

1 tbsp olive oil

1 onion, thinly sliced

1 red pepper, deseeded
and thinly sliced

2 tomatoes, peeled,
deseeded and chopped

6 large eggs

1 tbsp milk

2 tbsp finely grated
Parmesan cheese

salt and pepper

spanish omelette

Cook the potatoes in a saucepan of boiling water for
8–12 minutes until tender. Drain and leave to cool, then slice.

Heat the oil in an 18–20-cm/7–8-inch frying pan with a heatproof
handle and cook the sliced onion and red pepper until soft. Add
the tomatoes and cook for a further minute.

Add the potatoes to the pan and spread out evenly. Beat the
eggs, milk and cheese, and salt and pepper to taste, in a bowl
and pour over the potato mixture. Cook for 4–5 minutes until the
eggs are set underneath.

Meanwhile, preheat the grill to high. Place the frying pan under
the grill and cook the omelette for a further 3–4 minutes until
the eggs are set.

Leave to cool, then cut into wedges and wrap in foil for a lunch
box or spear onto cocktail sticks for a party snack.

serves 4

250 g/9 oz sushi rice

2 tbsp rice vinegar

1 tsp caster sugar

1/2 tsp salt

4 sheets nori

for the fillings

50 g/1³/4 oz smoked salmon

4-cm/1¹/2-inch piece cucumber, peeled, deseeded and cut into matchsticks

40 g/1¹/2 oz cooked peeled prawns

1 small avocado, stoned, peeled, thinly sliced and tossed in lemon juice

to serve

wasabi (Japanese horseradish sauce)

tamari (wheat-free soy sauce)

pink pickled ginger

mixed sushi rolls

Put the rice into a saucepan and cover with cold water. Bring to the boil, then reduce the heat, cover and simmer for 15–20 minutes, or until the rice is tender and the water has been absorbed. Drain if necessary and transfer to a bowl. Mix the vinegar, sugar and salt together, then, using a spatula, stir well into the rice. Cover with a damp cloth and leave to cool.

To make the rolls, lay a clean bamboo mat over a chopping board. Lay a sheet of nori, shiny-side down, on the mat. Spread a quarter of the rice mixture over the nori, using wet fingers to press it down evenly, leaving a 1-cm/1/2-inch margin at the top and bottom.

For smoked salmon and cucumber rolls, lay the salmon over the rice and arrange the cucumber in a line across the centre. For the prawn rolls, lay the prawns and avocado in a line across the centre.

Carefully hold the nearest edge of the mat, then, using the mat as a guide, roll up the nori tightly to make a neat tube of rice enclosing the filling. Seal the uncovered edge with a little water, then roll the sushi off the mat. Repeat to make 3 more rolls – you need 2 salmon and cucumber and 2 prawn and avocado in total.

Using a wet knife, cut each roll into 8 pieces and stand upright on a platter. Wipe and rinse the knife between cuts to prevent the rice from sticking. Serve the rolls with wasabi, tamari and pickled ginger.

makes 16

175 g/6 oz unsalted butter,
plus extra for greasing

3 tbsp clear honey

150 g/5$^1/_2$ oz demerara sugar

100 g/3$^1/_2$ oz smooth peanut
butter

225 g/8 oz porridge oats

50 g/1$^3/_4$ oz ready-to-eat
dried apricots, chopped

2 tbsp sunflower seeds

2 tbsp sesame seeds

sticky fruit flapjacks

Preheat the oven to 180°C/350°F/Gas Mark 4. Grease and line a
22-cm/8$^1/_2$-inch square baking tin.

Melt the butter, honey and sugar in a saucepan over a low
heat. When the sugar has melted, add the peanut butter and
stir until all the ingredients are well combined. Add all the
remaining ingredients and mix well.

Press the mixture into the prepared tin and bake in the
preheated oven for 20 minutes.

Remove from the oven and leave to cool in the tin, then cut
into 16 squares.

makes 10

150 g/5$^{1}/_{2}$ oz white plain flour

100 g/3$^{1}/_{2}$ oz light brown self-raising flour

1 tbsp oat bran

2 tsp baking powder

$^{1}/_{2}$ tsp bicarbonate of soda

pinch of salt

50 g/1$^{3}/_{4}$ oz demerara sugar

1 tbsp clear honey

1 large egg

200 ml/7 fl oz buttermilk

150 g/5$^{1}/_{2}$ oz fresh blueberries

blueberry bran muffins

Preheat the oven to 180°C/350°F/Gas Mark 4. Line 10 holes of a muffin tin with muffin paper cases.

Mix together the flours, bran, baking powder, bicarbonate of soda and salt in a bowl and stir in the sugar. Whisk together the honey, egg and buttermilk in together in a jug.

Pour the wet ingredients into the dry and stir briefly to combine. Don't overmix – the mixture should still be a little lumpy. Fold in the blueberries.

Spoon the mixture into the paper cases and bake in the preheated oven for 20 minutes until risen and lightly browned.

Remove the muffins from the oven and leave to cool in the tin. Serve warm or cold.

makes 1 loaf

unsalted butter, for
greasing

125 g/4¹/2 oz white
self-raising flour

100 g/3¹/2 oz light brown
self-raising flour

pinch of salt

¹/2 tsp ground cinnamon

¹/2 tsp ground nutmeg

150 g/5¹/2 oz demerara
sugar

2 large ripe bananas,
peeled

175 ml/6 fl oz orange
juice

2 eggs, beaten

4 tbsp rapeseed oil

honey, sliced banana
and chopped walnuts,
to serve

banana loaf

Preheat the oven to 180°C/350°F/Gas Mark 4. Lightly grease and
line a 450-g/1-lb loaf tin.

Sift the flours, salt and the spices into a large bowl. Stir in the
sugar.

In a separate bowl, mash the bananas with the orange juice,
then stir in the eggs and oil. Pour into the dry ingredients and
mix well.

Spoon into the prepared loaf tin and bake in the preheated oven
for 1 hour, then test to see if it is cooked by inserting a skewer
into the centre. If it comes out clean, the loaf is done. If not, bake
for a further 10 minutes and test again.

Remove from the oven and leave to cool in the tin. Turn the
loaf out, slice and serve with honey, sliced banana and chopped
walnuts.

Pizza

The word pizza comes from the Italian word 'pizzicare', meaning to be hot or spicy and it is thought that the original pizza consisted of a bread dough base drizzled liberally with olive oil and sprinkled with garlic, oregano and fiery hot peperoncino chillies. It was only in the nineteenth century, when the city of Naples created a pizza to honour Queen Margherita, that tomatoes and cheese – those staples of pizza toppings – were introduced. As Italians, particularly Neapolitans, moved across Europe and North America they opened pizzerias in all the major cities and this humble snack food became a global phenomenon.

Pizza toppings have become increasingly varied and interesting as cooks around the world have experimented with local ingredients. Modern toppings also tend to include more ingredients than the pizzas of the past. If Italy had a queen to honour now, tomatoes, cheese and basil would probably seem a somewhat inadequate way to commemorate a royal visit. Nevertheless, the classic recipes are still firm favourites with many, as they are quick and easy to prepare and the traditional flavour combinations have stood the test of time.

Making pizza

This book provides a recipe for basic Pizza Dough (see page 95) which takes little time, but it needs to stand for about 1 hour to rise. If you are in a hurry, you can use a ready-made, part-cooked pizza base. These are available from supermarkets and, while not quite as delicious as a home-made one, are still very satisfactory.

Many pizza recipes start by covering the pizza base with some kind of tomato sauce. One of the easiest

and most convenient options is to buy a good brand of ready-made pizza sauce. However, making your own is almost as easy. For a basic Tomato Sauce, soften a chopped onion and a finely chopped garlic clove in a tablespoon of olive oil in a saucepan for 5 minutes. Stir in 200 g/7 oz canned chopped tomatoes, 1–2 teaspoons tomato purée, a pinch of sugar and a pinch of dried oregano, season with salt and pepper and simmer gently, stirring occasionally, for 20–25 minutes, until thick and pulpy. Leave to cool completely before using.

Home-made tomato sauce can be stored in a screw-top jar in the refrigerator for up to a week. You could also use passata and even tomato purée, although this has a very intense flavour and is probably better diluted with a little water first. Peeled and finely diced fresh tomatoes may also be used,

creating a different texture. Of course, not all pizzas include tomatoes or tomato sauce.

The recipes in this section suggest a huge variety of different toppings to suit all tastes. They are all easy to follow and have been divided into four chapters, making it easy to find exactly the one you want. Classic Toppings speaks for itself and includes traditional meat, vegetarian and shellfish pizzas. The toppings in Meat Lovers range from creamy chicken to spicy pepperoni and meatballs – the perfect choice when you're really hungry. Strictly Vegetarian suggests some delicious new ways with vegetables as well as some favourite combinations, while the recipes in Something Special are ideal for those days when you want something a little different.

Classic Toppings

serves 2–4

15 g/$^1/_2$ oz fresh yeast or
1 tsp dried or active dry yeast

6 tbsp lukewarm water

$^1/_2$ tsp sugar

1 tbsp olive oil, plus extra
for oiling

175 g/6 oz plain flour, plus
extra for dusting

1 tsp salt

pizza dough

Combine the fresh yeast with the water and sugar in a bowl.
If using dried yeast, sprinkle it over the surface of the water
(without the sugar) and whisk in until dissolved.

Set aside in a warm place for 10–15 minutes until frothy on the
surface. Stir in the olive oil.

Sift the flour and salt into a large bowl. If using easy-blend yeast,
stir it in. Make a well in the centre and pour in the yeast liquid.

Using either floured hands or a wooden spoon, mix together to
form a dough. Turn out onto a floured work surface and knead
for about 5 minutes or until smooth and elastic.

Place the dough in a large oiled plastic bag and set aside in a
warm place for about 1 hour or until doubled in size. Airing
cupboards are often the best places for this process, as the
temperature remains constant.

Turn out onto a lightly floured surface and 'knock back' by
punching the dough. This releases any air bubbles which would
make the pizza uneven. Knead 4 or 5 times. The dough is now
ready to use.

serves 2–4

2 tbsp olive oil, plus extra
for brushing

1 quantity Pizza Dough
(see page 95), or 1 x 25-cm/
10-inch pizza base

plain flour, for dusting

6 tomatoes, thinly sliced

175 g/6 oz mozzarella cheese,
drained and thinly sliced

2 tbsp shredded fresh basil
leaves

salt and pepper

Margherita pizza

Preheat the oven to 230°C/450°F/Gas Mark 8. Brush a baking
sheet with oil.

Roll out the dough on a lightly floured surface to a 25-cm/
10-inch round. Place on the baking sheet and push up the edge
a little. Cover and let stand in a warm place for 10 minutes.

Arrange the tomato and mozzarella slices alternately over the
pizza base. Season to taste with salt and pepper, sprinkle with
the basil, and drizzle with the olive oil.

Bake in the oven for 15–20 minutes, until the crust is crisp and
the cheese has melted.

serves 2–4

2 tbsp olive oil, plus extra for
brushing

1 quantity Pizza Dough
(see page 95), or 1 x 25-cm/
10-inch pizza base

plain flour, for dusting

400 g/14 oz canned chopped
tomatoes

140 g/5 oz ham, diced

200 g/7 oz canned pineapple
slices in juice, drained

55 g/2 oz Cheddar cheese,
grated

Hawaiian pizza

Preheat the oven to 200°C/400°F/Gas Mark 6. Brush a baking
sheet with oil.

Roll out the dough on a lightly floured surface to a 25-cm/
10-inch round. Place on the baking sheet and push up the edge
a little. Cover and let stand in a warm place for 10 minutes.

Spoon the tomatoes over the base almost to the edge, then
sprinkle evenly with the ham.

Cut the pineapple slices into bite-sized pieces and sprinkle
them over the pizza. Sprinkle with the grated cheese and
bake for 20 minutes, until the edge is crisp and golden. Serve
immediately.

serves 4

2 loaves of ciabatta or
2 baguettes

1 quantity basic Tomato
Sauce (see page 91)

4 plum tomatoes, thinly
sliced lengthways

150 g/5½ oz mozzarella
cheese, thinly sliced

10 black olives, cut into rings

8 fresh basil leaves, shredded

olive oil, for drizzling

salt and pepper

tomato & olive pizzas

Cut the bread in half lengthways and lightly toast the cut side of the bread. Carefully spread the toasted bread with the Tomato Sauce.

Arrange the tomato and mozzarella slices alternately along the length of each toasted slice.

Top with the olive rings and half of the basil. Drizzle over a little olive oil and season with salt and pepper.

Either place under a preheated medium grill and cook until the cheese is melted and bubbling, or bake in an oven preheated to 200°C/400°F/Gas Mark 6 for 15–20 minutes.

Sprinkle over the remaining basil and serve immediately.

serves 2–4

olive oil, for brushing

1 quantity Pizza Dough (see page 95), or 1 x 25-cm/ 10-inch pizza base

plain flour, for dusting

2 tbsp butter or margarine

350 g/12 oz mixed mushrooms, sliced

2 garlic cloves, crushed

2 tbsp chopped fresh parsley, plus extra to garnish

2 tbsp tomato purée

6 tbsp passata

85 g/3 oz mozzarella cheese, grated

salt and pepper

garlic mushroom pizza

Preheat the oven to 190°C/375°F/Gas Mark 5. Brush a baking sheet with oil.

Roll out the dough on a lightly floured surface to a 25-cm/ 10-inch round. Place on the baking sheet and push up the edge a little. Cover and let stand in a warm place for 10 minutes.

Melt the butter in a frying pan and cook the mushrooms, garlic and parsley together over a low heat for 5 minutes.

Combine the tomato purée and passata and spoon onto the pizza base, leaving a 1-cm/½-inch edge of dough. Spoon the mushroom mixture on top. Season to taste with salt and pepper and sprinkle the cheese on top.

Cook the pizza in the oven for 20–25 minutes or until the base is crisp and the cheese has melted. Garnish with chopped parsley and serve immediately.

serves 2–4

4 tbsp olive oil, plus extra for brushing

140 g/5 oz mushrooms, chopped

1 garlic clove, thinly sliced (optional)

1 tbsp lemon juice

1 quantity Pizza Dough (see page 95), or 1 x 25-cm/ 10-inch pizza base

plain flour, for dusting

140 g/5 oz bacon, diced

pinch of dried oregano

55 g/2 oz Cheddar cheese, grated

salt and pepper

tasty bacon pizza

Heat half the olive oil in a saucepan. Add the mushrooms, garlic and lemon juice, season with salt and pepper, cover and cook over a low heat, stirring occasionally, for 6 minutes. Remove the pan from the heat and leave to cool.

Preheat the oven to 200°C/400°F/Gas Mark 6. Brush a baking sheet with oil.

Roll out the dough on a lightly floured surface to a 25-cm/ 10-inch round. Place on the baking sheet and push up the edge a little. Cover and leave to stand in a warm place for 10 minutes.

Brush the pizza base with half the remaining olive oil and spread out the mushrooms evenly on top almost to the edge. Sprinkle with the diced bacon and season with a pinch of dried oregano. Sprinkle the cheese over the pizza, drizzle with the remaining oil and bake for 20–25 minutes, until crisp and golden. Serve immediately.

serves 2–4

2 tbsp olive oil, plus extra for brushing

1 quantity Pizza Dough (see page 95), or 1 x 25-cm/ 10-inch pizza base

plain flour, for dusting

175 ml/6 fl oz passata or 1 quantity basic Tomato Sauce (see page 91)

1 red onion, halved and thinly sliced

55 g/2 oz Parmesan cheese, freshly grated

55 g/2 oz Gorgonzola cheese

55 g/2 oz fontina cheese, thinly sliced

55 g/2 oz goat's cheese

1 tbsp pine kernels or capers

salt and pepper

fresh basil sprigs, to garnish

quattro formaggi pizza

Preheat the oven to 200°C/400°F/Gas Mark 6. Brush a baking sheet with oil.

Roll out the dough on a lightly floured surface to a 25-cm/ 10-inch round. Place on the baking sheet and push up the edge a little. Cover and leave to stand in a warm place for 10 minutes.

Brush the pizza base with half the olive oil, then spread the passata or Tomato Sauce over it almost to the edge. Spread out the onion slices evenly over the top and season with salt and pepper.

Cover one quarter of the pizza base with grated Parmesan. Crumble the Gorgonzola over a second quarter and arrange the slices of fontina over a third quarter. Depending on the type of goat's cheese, either crumble it directly over the remaining quarter or slice it first before adding to the pizza.

Sprinkle the pine kernels over the top and drizzle with the remaining olive oil. Bake for 20–25 minutes, until crisp and golden. Garnish with basil sprigs and serve immediately.

serves 2–4

3 tbsp olive oil, plus extra for brushing and drizzling

1 quantity Pizza Dough (see page 95), or 1 x 25-cm/ 10-inch pizza base

plain flour, for dusting

1 quantity basic Tomato Sauce (see page 91)

2 tbsp freshly grated Parmesan cheese

175 g/6 oz fresh spinach

1 small red onion, thinly sliced

1/4 tsp freshly grated nutmeg

2 hard-boiled eggs

15 g/1/2 oz fresh white breadcrumbs

55 g/2 oz Jarlsberg, Cheddar or Gruyère cheese, grated

2 tbsp flaked almonds

salt and pepper

Florentine pizza

Preheat the oven to 200°C/400°F/Gas Mark 6. Brush a baking sheet with oil.

Roll out the dough on a lightly floured surface to a 25-cm/ 10-inch round. Place on the baking sheet and push up the edge a little. Cover and let stand in a warm place for 10 minutes. Spread the Tomato Sauce almost to the edge and sprinkle the Parmesan over it.

Remove the stalks from the spinach and wash the leaves thoroughly in plenty of cold water. Drain well and pat off the excess water with kitchen paper.

Heat the remaining oil and cook the onion for 5 minutes until softened. Add the spinach and cook until just wilted. Drain off any excess liquid. Arrange on the pizza and sprinkle over the nutmeg and sprinkle the Parmesan over it.

Shell and slice the eggs. Arrange the slices of egg on top of the spinach.

Combine the breadcrumbs, cheese and almonds, and sprinkle over. Drizzle with a little olive oil and season to taste.

Bake for 18–20 minutes, or until the edge is crisp and golden. Serve the pizza immediately.

serves 2–4

2 tbsp olive oil, plus extra for brushing

1 quantity Pizza Dough (see page 95), or 1 x 25-cm/ 10-inch pizza base

plain flour, for dusting

400 g/14 oz canned chopped tomatoes

200 g/7 oz canned tuna in olive oil, drained

140 g/5 oz cooked peeled prawns

100 g/3½ oz mozzarella cheese, grated

1 tbsp chopped fresh parsley

1 tbsp chopped fresh oregano

1 garlic clove, very finely chopped

seafood pizza

Preheat the oven to 200°C/400°F/Gas Mark 6. Brush a baking sheet with oil.

Roll out the dough on a lightly floured surface to a 25-cm/ 10-inch round. Place on the baking sheet and push up the edge a little. Cover and let stand in a warm place for 10 minutes.

Spoon the tomatoes evenly over the base almost to the edge. Flake the tuna and spread it over the tomatoes, then arrange the prawns on top. Sprinkle with the mozzarella.

Mix together the parsley, oregano, garlic and olive oil, and drizzle the mixture over the pizza. Bake for 20 minutes, until the edge is crisp and golden. Serve immediately.

Meat Lovers

serves 2–4

olive oil, for brushing and
drizzling

1 quantity Pizza Dough
(see page 95), or 1 x 25-cm/
10-inch pizza base

plain flour, for dusting

4 tbsp sundried tomato paste

4 tomatoes, skinned and
thinly sliced

2 red onions, finely chopped

4 slices prosciutto or other
cooked ham, coarsely
shredded

12 slices pepperoni sausage

12 black olives

3/4 tsp dried oregano

55 g/2 oz mozzarella cheese,
grated

salt

pepperoni & onion pizza

Preheat the oven to 220°C/425°F/Gas Mark 7. Brush a baking
sheet with oil.

Roll out the dough on a lightly floured surface to a 25-cm/
10-inch round. Place on the baking sheet and push up the edge
a little. Cover and let stand in a warm place for 10 minutes.

Spread the sun-dried tomato paste evenly over the base. Arrange
the tomato slices on the base and season with salt. Sprinkle over
the chopped onion and prosciutto and arrange the pepperoni
on top. Add the olives and sprinkle with oregano. Then add the
grated cheese, and drizzle with olive oil.

Bake in the oven for 20–30 minutes, until golden and sizzling.
Serve immediately.

serves 2–4

4 tbsp olive oil, plus extra for brushing

1 quantity Pizza Dough (see page 95), or 1 x 25-cm/ 10-inch pizza base

plain flour, for dusting

2 shallots, thinly sliced

1 yellow pepper, deseeded and cut into thin strips

115 g/4 oz chestnut mushrooms, thinly sliced

350 g/12 oz skinless, boneless chicken breasts portions, cut into thin strips

2 tbsp chopped fresh parsley

175 g/6 oz mozzarella cheese, grated

salt and pepper

chicken & mushroom pizza

Preheat the oven to 200°C/400°F/Gas Mark 6. Brush a baking sheet with oil.

Roll out the dough on a lightly floured surface to a 25-cm/ 10-inch round. Place on the baking sheet and push up the edge a little. Cover and let stand in a warm place for 10 minutes.

Heat 2 tablespoons of olive oil in a wok or large frying pan. Add the shallots, yellow pepper, mushrooms and chicken, and stir-fry over a medium–high heat for 4–5 minutes. Remove the mixture with a slotted spoon and leave to cool.

Brush the pizza with 1 tablespoon of olive oil. Stir the parsley into the chicken and mushroom mixture and season with salt and pepper. Spread the mixture evenly over the pizza base almost to the edge. Sprinkle with the mozzarella, drizzle over the remaining olive oil, and bake for 20 minutes, until the edge is crisp and golden. Serve immediately.

serves 2–4

2 tbsp olive oil, plus extra for brushing

1 quantity Pizza Dough (see page 95), or 1 x 25-cm/ 10-inch pizza base

plain flour, for dusting

200 g/7 oz chorizo or other spicy sausages

55 g/2 oz freshly grated Parmesan cheese

400 g/14 oz canned chopped tomatoes

115 g/4 oz pancetta or bacon, cut into thin slices

1 tbsp fresh basil leaves

sausage pizza

Preheat the oven to 200°C/400°F/Gas Mark 6. Brush a baking sheet with oil.

Roll out the dough on a lightly floured surface to a 25-cm/ 10-inch round. Place on the baking sheet and push up the edge a little. Cover and let stand in a warm place for 10 minutes.

Remove and discard the sausage casings and crumble the meat into a bowl. Add the Parmesan and mix well.

Spoon the tomatoes evenly over the pizza base almost to the edge, then sprinkle with the sausage mixture. Top with the pancetta and basil leaves, and drizzle with the olive oil. Bake for 20 minutes, until the edge is crisp and golden. Serve immediately.

serves 2–4

2 tbsp olive oil, plus extra for brushing

1 bunch of spring onions, chopped

2 garlic cloves, finely chopped

225g/8 oz minced beef

1 tsp chilli powder

200 g/7 oz canned chopped tomatoes

1/2 tsp Tabasco sauce

200 g/7 oz canned red kidney beans, drained and rinsed

1 quantity Pizza Dough (see page 95), or 1 x 25-cm/ 10-inch pizza base

plain flour, for dusting

2–3 jalapeño chillies, thinly sliced

150 g/5 oz mozzarella cheese, grated

salt and pepper

chilli pizza

Heat the oil in a saucepan. Add the spring onions and cook over a medium–low heat, stirring occasionally, for 4–5 minutes, until softened. Add the garlic, minced beef and chilli powder and cook, stirring occasionally, for 5 minutes, until browned. Stir in the tomatoes and Tabasco and bring to the boil. Lower the heat, cover and simmer for 30 minutes, then remove the pan from the heat, stir in the kidney beans, season with salt and pepper and leave to cool.

Preheat the oven to 200°C/400°F/Gas Mark 6. Brush a baking sheet with oil.

Roll out the dough on a lightly floured surface to a 10-inch/ 25-cm round. Place on the baking sheet and push up the edge a little. Cover and let stand in a warm place for 10 minutes.

Spoon the meat mixture evenly over the pizza base almost to the edge. Sprinkle with the chillies and mozzarella and bake for 20 minutes, until the edge is crisp and golden. Serve immediately.

serves 2–4

2 tbsp olive oil, plus extra for brushing

1 quantity Pizza Dough (see page 95), or 1 x 25-cm/ 10-inch pizza base

plain flour, for dusting

2 tbsp sun-dried tomato paste

150 g/5 oz mozzarella cheese, torn into small pieces

400 g/14 oz canned chopped tomatoes

70 g/2½ oz ham, cut into thin strips

2 garlic cloves, finely chopped

½ red pepper, deseeded and thinly sliced

6 stoned black olives, halved

1 tbsp fresh basil leaves

2 tbsp freshly grated Parmesan cheese

ham & tomato pizza

Preheat the oven to 200°C/400°F/Gas Mark 6. Brush a baking sheet with oil.

Roll out the dough on a lightly floured surface to a 25-cm/ 10-inch round. Place on the baking sheet and push up the edge a little. Cover and let stand in a warm place for 10 minutes.

Spread the sun-dried tomato paste over the base almost to the edge. Sprinkle with half the mozzarella. Spoon the tomatoes evenly over the top, then sprinkle with the ham, garlic, red pepper, olives and basil leaves.

Add the remaining mozzarella, drizzle with the olive oil and sprinkle evenly with the Parmesan. Bake for 20 minutes, until the edge is crisp and golden. Serve immediately.

serves 2–4

250 g/9 oz flaky pastry dough, well chilled

plain flour, for dusting

3 tbsp butter

1 red onion, chopped

1 garlic clove, chopped

5 tbsp plain white flour

300 ml/10 fl oz milk

50 g/1¾ oz finely grated Parmesan cheese, plus extra for sprinkling

2 eggs, hard-boiled, cut into quarters

100 g/3½ oz Italian pork sausage, such as Felino salami, cut into strips

salt and pepper

fresh thyme sprigs, to garnish

mini creamy ham pizzas

Fold the pastry in half and grate it into 4 individual flan tins measuring 10 cm/4 inches across. Using a floured fork, press the pastry flakes down evenly, making sure that there are no holes and that the pastry comes up the sides of the tins.

Line with foil and bake blind in a preheated oven, 220°C/425°F/ Gas Mark 7, for 10 minutes. Reduce the heat to 200°C/400°F/Gas Mark 6, remove the foil and cook for a further 15 minutes, or until golden and set.

Heat the butter in a saucepan. Add the onion and garlic and cook for 5–6 minutes, or until softened.

Add the flour, stirring well to coat the onion and garlic. Gradually stir in the milk to make a thick sauce.

Season the sauce with salt and pepper to taste, then stir in the Parmesan. Do not reheat once the cheese has been added or the sauce will become too stringy.

Spread the sauce over the cooked pastry cases. Decorate with the eggs and strips of sausage.

Sprinkle with a little extra Parmesan, return to the oven and bake for 5 minutes, just to heat through.

Serve immediately, garnished with sprigs of fresh thyme.

serves 2–4

2 tbsp olive oil, plus extra for brushing

2–4 fresh or pickled jalapeño chillies, thinly sliced

1 quantity Pizza Dough (see page 95), or 1 x 25-cm/10-inch pizza base

plain flour, for dusting

125–175 ml/4–6 fl oz smoky barbecue sauce

4 tomatoes, sliced

85 g/3 oz smoked ham, diced

85 g/3 oz pepperoni, thinly sliced

55 g/2 oz Gruyère cheese, grated

salt

Chicago pepperoni pizza

Preheat the oven to 200°C/400°F/Gas Mark 6. Brush a baking sheet with oil. Deseed the chillies if you prefer a milder flavour.

Roll out the dough on a lightly floured surface to a 25-cm/10-inch round. Place on the baking sheet and push up the edge a little. Cover and leave to stand in a warm place for 10 minutes.

Brush the pizza base with half the oil, then spread the barbecue sauce evenly over it almost to the edge. Arrange the tomato slices over the base and season with salt, then sprinkle with the smoked ham. Cover with the pepperoni slices, top with the chillies and sprinkle with the cheese. Drizzle with the remaining oil and bake for 20–25 minutes, until crisp and golden. Serve immediately.

serves 2–4

4 tbsp olive oil, plus extra for
brushing

55 g/2 oz smoked bacon,
diced

1 onion, finely chopped

280 g/10 oz skinless and
boneless chicken breast
portions, cut into strips

1 tsp chopped fresh tarragon

115 g/4 oz sliced smoked
chicken, cut into strips

1½ quantity Pizza Dough
(see page 95), or 1 x 38-cm/
15-inch pizza base

plain flour for dusting

pinch of dried oregano

140 g/5 oz mozzarella cheese,
grated

deep-pan chicken feast pizza

Heat 2 tablespoons of the oil with the bacon in a frying pan. Add the onion and cook over a low heat, stirring occasionally, for 5 minutes, until softened. Add the fresh chicken strips, increase the heat to medium and stir-fry for 4–5 minutes, until lightly browned on the outside.

Remove the pan from the heat and drain off as much oil as possible. Stir in the tarragon and leave to cool completely. Then add the smoked chicken strips.

Preheat the oven to 220°C/425°F/Gas Mark 7. Brush a baking sheet or deep pizza pan with oil.

Roll out the dough on a lightly floured surface to a 38-cm/ 15-inch round. Place on the baking sheet, push up the edge and roll it over a little. Cover and leave to stand in a warm place for 10 minutes.

Brush the pizza base with 1 tablespoon of oil, then spoon on the chicken mixture and sprinkle with the oregano. Drizzle with the remaining oil and sprinkle with the mozzarella. Bake for 25–30 minutes, until golden. Serve immediately.

serves 2–4

5 tbsp olive oil, plus extra for brushing

2 onions, thinly sliced

200 g/7 oz lean minced beef

25 g/1 oz ham, finely chopped

1 tbsp chopped fresh flat-leaf parsley

55 g/2 oz Parmesan cheese, grated

1 egg yolk

1 quantity Pizza Dough (see page 95), or 1 x 25-cm/ 10-inch pizza base

1 quantity basic Tomato Sauce (see page 91)

8 black olives

115 g/4 oz mozzarella cheese, grated

salt and pepper

for the béchamel sauce

40 g/1½ oz butter

1 tbsp plain flour, plus extra for dusting

125 ml/4 fl oz milk

pinch of grated nutmeg

meatball pizza

Preheat the oven to 200°C/400°F/Gas Mark 6. Brush a baking sheet with oil. Heat 2 tablespoons of the oil in a frying pan. Add the onions and cook over a low heat, stirring occasionally, for 15–20 minutes, until golden brown.

Meanwhile, make a béchamel sauce; melt 1 tablespoon of the butter in a small saucepan. Stir in the flour and cook, stirring constantly, for 1 minute. Gradually stir in the milk and bring to the boil, stirring constantly. Cook, stirring, for 1–2 minutes more, until thickened. Remove the pan from the heat and stir in a small pinch of nutmeg.

Mix together the minced beef, ham, parsley, Parmesan and egg yolk in a bowl and season. Add 1–2 tablespoons of the béchamel and bring the mixture together. Shape into about 12 small balls and dust lightly with flour. Melt the remaining butter with 1 tablespoon of the remaining oil in another frying pan. Add the meatballs and cook over a medium heat, turning frequently, for 4–5 minutes, until browned all over. Remove with a slotted spoon and set aside.

Roll out the dough on a lightly floured surface to a 25-cm/ 10-inch round. Place on the baking sheet and push up the edge a little. Cover and leave to stand in a warm place for 10 minutes.

Brush the pizza base with half the remaining olive oil. Spread the Tomato Sauce over the base almost to the edge. Using a slotted spoon, sprinkle the onions evenly over the top. Arrange the meatballs on top of the onions and add the olives, then sprinkle with the mozzarella and drizzle with the remaining oil. Bake for 20 minutes, until crisp and golden. Serve immediately.

Strictly Vegetarian

serves 2–4

125 ml/4 fl oz olive oil, plus
extra for brushing

4 garlic cloves

2 red onions, cut into wedges

1 orange pepper, deseeded
and cut into 8 strips

1 yellow pepper, deseeded
and cut into 8 strips

4 baby courgettes, halved
lengthways

4 baby aubergines, cut
lengthways into 4 slices

1 tbsp balsamic vinegar

2 tbsp fresh basil leaves

1 quantity Pizza Dough
(see page 95), or 1 x 25-cm/
10-inch pizza base

plain flour, for dusting

1 quantity basic Tomato
Sauce (see page 91)

175 g/6 oz goat's cheese,
diced

salt and pepper

roasted vegetable pizza

Preheat the oven to 200°C/400°F/Gas Mark 6. Brush a baking
sheet with oil.

Spread the garlic, onions, peppers, courgettes and aubergines in
a roasting tin. Season to taste with salt and pepper. Mix together
the oil, vinegar and basil in a jug and pour the mixture over the
vegetables, tossing well to coat. Roast in the preheated oven for
15 minutes, turning once or twice during cooking. Leave to cool.
Increase the oven temperature to 220°C/425°F/Gas Mark 7.

Roll out the dough on a lightly floured surface to a 25-cm/
10-inch round. Place on the baking sheet and push up the edge a
little. Cover and let stand in a warm place for 10 minutes.

Add the Tomato Sauce to the pizza base, spreading it almost
to the edges. Peel off the skins from the pepper strips. Peel and
slice the garlic. Arrange the vegetables on top of the Tomato
Sauce, then sprinkle with the goat's cheese. Drizzle over the
roasting juices.

Bake for 15–20 minutes, or until golden. Garnish with fresh basil
and serve immediately.

serves 8

1 quantity Pizza Dough (see page 95) or 1 x 25-cm/ 10-inch pizza base

plain flour, for dusting

2 tbsp olive oil, plus extra for oiling and drizzling

1/2 red pepper, deseeded and thinly sliced

1/2 green pepper, deseeded and thinly sliced

1/2 yellow pepper, deseeded and thinly sliced

1 small red onion, thinly sliced

1 garlic clove, crushed

1 quantity basic Tomato Sauce (see page 91)

3 tbsp sultanas

4 tbsp pine kernels

1 tbsp chopped fresh thyme

salt and pepper

pepper & onion pizza fingers

Preheat the oven to 200°C/400°F/Gas Mark 6.

Roll out or press the dough, using a rolling pin or your hands, on a lightly floured surface to fit a 30 x 18-cm/12 x 7-inch oiled Swiss roll tin. Place the dough in the tin and push up the edges slightly.

Cover with clingfilm and set the dough aside in a warm place for about 10 minutes to rise slightly.

Heat the oil in a large frying pan. Add the peppers, onion and garlic and cook gently for 5 minutes until they have softened. Set aside to cool.

Spread the Tomato Sauce over the base of the pizza almost to the edge. Sprinkle over the sultanas and top with the cooled pepper mixture. Add the pine kernels and thyme. Drizzle with a little olive oil and season to taste with salt and pepper.

Bake for 18–20 minutes, or until the edges are crisp and golden. Cut into fingers and serve immediately.

serves 2–4

3 tbsp oil, plus extra for brushing

1 quantity Pizza Dough (see page 95), or 1 x 25-cm/ 10-inch pizza base

plain flour, for dusting

2 garlic cloves, crushed

2 tbsp chopped fresh oregano

85 g/3 oz curd cheese

1 tbsp milk

40 g/1½ oz butter

350 g/12 oz mixed mushrooms, sliced

2 tsp lemon juice

1 tbsp chopped fresh marjoram

4 tbsp freshly grated Parmesan cheese

salt and pepper

mixed mushroom pizza

Preheat the oven to 240°C/475°F/Gas Mark 9. Brush a baking sheet with oil.

Roll out the dough on a lightly floured surface to a 25-cm/ 10-inch round. Place on the baking sheet and push up the edge a little. Cover and let stand in a warm place for 10 minutes.

Mix together 2 tablespoons of the oil, the garlic and oregano and brush over the pizza base.

Mix together the curd cheese and milk in a bowl. Season to taste with salt and pepper and spread the mixture over the pizza base, leaving a 4-cm/1½-inch border.

Heat the butter and remaining oil together in a large frying pan. Add the mushrooms and cook over a high heat for 2 minutes. Remove the frying pan from the heat, season to taste with salt and pepper and stir in the lemon juice and marjoram.

Spoon the mushroom mixture over the pizza base, leaving a 1-cm/½-inch border. Sprinkle with the grated Parmesan, then bake in the oven for 12–15 minutes, until the crusts are crisp and the mushrooms are cooked. Serve immediately.

serves 2–4

olive oil, for brushing

1 quantity Pizza Dough
(see page 95), or 1 x 25-cm/
10-inch pizza base

plain flour, for dusting

4 tbsp sun-dried tomato
paste

150g/5^{1}/$_{2}$ oz ricotta cheese

10 sun-dried tomatoes in oil,
drained

1 tbsp fresh thyme

salt and pepper

tomato & ricotta pizza

Preheat the oven to 200°C/400°F/Gas Mark 6. Brush a baking sheet with oil.

Roll out the dough on a lightly floured surface to a 25-cm/ 10-inch round. Place on the baking sheet and push up the edge a little. Cover and let stand in a warm place for 10 minutes.

Spread the sun-dried tomato paste evenly over the dough, then dot spoonfuls of ricotta cheese on top.

Cut the sun-dried tomatoes into thin strips and arrange these over the top of the pizza.

Finally, sprinkle the fresh thyme leaves over the top of the pizza and season with salt and pepper to taste. Bake for 30 minutes or until the crust is golden. Serve immediately.

serves 4

1 quantity Pizza Dough
(see page 95), or 1 x 25-cm/
10-inch pizza base

olive oil, for brushing

200 g/7 oz canned chopped
tomatoes with garlic and
herbs

2 tbsp tomato paste

200 g/7 oz canned red kidney
beans, drained and rinsed

115 g/4 oz sweetcorn kernels,
thawed if frozen

1–2 tsp chilli sauce

1 large red onion, shredded

100 g/3½ oz mature Cheddar
cheese, grated

1 large, fresh green chilli,
deseeded and sliced into
rings

salt and pepper

Mexican pizza

Preheat the oven to 200°C/400°F/Gas Mark 6. Brush a baking sheet with oil.

Roll out the dough on a lightly floured surface to a 25-cm/ 10-inch round. Place on the baking sheet and push up the edge a little. Cover and let stand in a warm place for 10 minutes.

Mix together the chopped tomatoes, tomato paste, kidney beans and sweetcorn in a bowl and add chilli sauce to taste. Season with salt and pepper.

Spread the tomato and kidney bean mixture evenly over the pizza base. Top the pizza with shredded onion and sprinkle with some grated Cheddar cheese and a few slices of green chilli, to taste.

Bake for about 20 minutes, until the vegetables are tender, the cheese has melted and the base is crisp and golden.

Remove the pizza from the baking tray and transfer to serving plates. Serve immediately.

serves 2–4

olive oil, for brushing and drizzling

1 quantity Pizza Dough (see page 95), or 1 x 25-cm/ 10-inch pizza base

plain flour, for dusting

6 spinach leaves

1 quantity basic Tomato Sauce (see page 91)

1 tomato, sliced

1 celery stick, thinly sliced

1/2 green pepper, deseeded and thinly sliced

1 baby courgette, sliced

25 g/1 oz asparagus tips

25 g/1 oz sweetcorn, thawed if frozen

4 tbsp peas, thawed if frozen

4 spring onions, trimmed and chopped

1 tbsp chopped fresh mixed herbs

55 g/2 oz mozzarella cheese, grated

2 tbsp freshly grated Parmesan cheese

1 artichoke heart

salt and pepper

vegetable pizza

Preheat the oven to 200°C/400°F/Gas Mark 6. Brush a baking sheet with oil.

Roll out the dough on a lightly floured surface to a 25-cm/ 10-inch round. Place on the baking sheet and push up the edge a little. Cover and let stand in a warm place for 10 minutes.

Remove the stalks from the spinach and wash the leaves in cold water. Pat dry with kitchen paper.

Spread the Tomato Sauce over the base of the pizza almost to the edge. Arrange the spinach leaves on top of the sauce, followed by the tomato slices. Top with the remaining vegetables and the fresh mixed herbs.

Combine the cheeses and sprinkle over the pizza. Place the artichoke heart in the centre. Drizzle the pizza with a little olive oil and season to taste.

Bake in the oven for 18–20 minutes or until the edge is crisp and golden brown. Serve immediately.

serves 2–4

55 g/2 oz sun-dried tomatoes
in oil, drained and coarsely
chopped

4 tbsp pine kernels

25 g/1 oz fresh basil leaves

1 garlic clove, chopped

5 tbsp olive oil, plus extra for
brushing

2 tbsp grated Parmesan
cheese

1 quantity Pizza Dough
(see page 95), or 1 x 25-cm/
10-inch pizza base

plain flour, for dusting

85 g/3 oz goat's cheese

85 g/3 oz red cherry
tomatoes, halved

85 g/3 oz yellow cherry
tomatoes, halved

basil, to garnish

salt and pepper

goat's cheese & sun-dried tomato pizza

Put the sun-dried tomatoes, pine kernels, basil and garlic
in a food processor or blender and process to a purée. With
the motor running, gradually add the olive oil through the
feeder tube or hole until thoroughly combined. Scrape into a
bowl and stir in the Parmesan. Alternatively, pound the sun-
dried tomatoes, pine kernels, basil and garlic to a paste in a
mortar with a pestle. Gradually beat in the oil, then stir in the
Parmesan. Season lightly with salt and pepper.

Preheat the oven to 200°C/400°F/Gas Mark 6. Brush a baking
sheet with oil.

Roll out the dough on a lightly floured surface to a 25-cm/
10-inch round. Place on the baking sheet and push up the edge
a little. Cover and leave to stand in a warm place for 10 minutes.

Spread the sun-dried tomato mixture over the pizza base almost
to the edge. Crumble the goat's cheese over it and arrange the
tomato halves on top, cut sides up. Bake for 20 minutes, until
crisp and golden. Garnish with basil and serve immediately.

serves 2–4

2 tbsp olive oil, plus extra for brushing and drizzling

1 quantity Pizza Dough (see page 95), or 1 x 25-cm/ 10-inch pizza base

plain flour, for dusting

350 g/12 oz spinach

1 onion, thinly sliced

6 tbsp ricotta cheese

1/2 tsp freshly grated nutmeg

2 tbsp pine kernels

115 g/4 oz Fontina cheese, sliced thinly

salt and pepper

ricotta, spinach & pine kernel pizza

Preheat the oven to 220°C/425°F/Gas Mark 7. Brush a baking sheet with oil.

Roll out the dough on a lightly floured surface to a 25-cm/ 10-inch round. Place on the baking sheet and push up the edge a little. Cover and let stand in a warm place for 10 minutes.

Wash the spinach in cold water and dry well. Heat the oil in a pan, add the onion and cook until soft and translucent. Add the spinach and cook, stirring, until just wilted. Remove the pan from the heat and drain off any liquid.

Spread the ricotta cheese evenly over the pizza base, then cover with the spinach and onion mixture. Sprinkle over the nutmeg and pine kernels and season to taste with salt and pepper. Top with the slices of Fontina and drizzle with olive oil. Bake in the oven for 20–30 minutes, until golden and sizzling. Serve immediately.

serves 2–4

2 tbsp olive oil, plus extra for brushing and drizzling

1 quantity Pizza Dough (see page 95), or 1 x 25-cm/ 10-inch pizza base

plain flour, for dusting

1 quantity basic Tomato Sauce (see page 91)

115 g/4 oz soft cheese

1 tbsp chopped fresh mixed herbs, such as parsley, oregano and basil

225 g/8 oz wild mushrooms, such as oyster, shiitake or ceps, or 115 g/4 oz each wild and button mushrooms

1/4 tsp fennel seeds

4 tbsp roughly chopped walnuts

40 g/11/2 oz blue cheese, of choice

salt and pepper

mushroom & walnut pizza

Preheat the oven to 200°C/400°F/Gas Mark 6. Brush a baking sheet with oil.

Roll out the dough on a lightly floured surface to a 25-cm/ 10-inch round. Place on the baking sheet and push up the edge a little. Cover and let stand in a warm place for 10 minutes.

Carefully spread the Tomato Sauce almost to the edge of the pizza base. Dot with the soft cheese and chopped fresh herbs.

Wipe and slice the mushrooms. Heat the oil in a large frying pan or wok and stir-fry the mushrooms and fennel seeds for 2–3 minutes. Spread over the pizza with the walnuts.

Crumble the blue cheese over the pizza, drizzle with a little olive oil and season with salt and pepper to taste.

Bake in the oven for 18–20 minutes or until the edge is crisp and golden. Serve immediately.

Something
Special

makes 4

2 tbsp olive oil, plus extra for brushing

1 red onion, thinly sliced

1 garlic clove, chopped finely

400 g/14 oz canned tomatoes, chopped

55 g/2 oz black olives, stoned

2 quantities Pizza Dough, combined (see page 95)

plain flour, for dusting

200 g/7 oz mozzarella cheese, drained and diced

1 tbsp chopped fresh oregano

salt and pepper

pizza turnovers

Preheat the oven to 200°C/400°F/Gas Mark 6. Brush two baking sheets with oil.

To make the filling, heat the olive oil in a frying pan. Add the onion and garlic and cook over a low heat, stirring occasionally, for 5 minutes, until softened. Add the tomatoes and cook, stirring occasionally, for a further 5 minutes. Stir in the olives and season to taste with salt and pepper. Remove the frying pan from the heat.

Divide the dough into 4 pieces. Roll out each piece on a lightly floured surface to form a 20-cm/8-inch round.

Divide the tomato mixture between the rounds, spreading it over half of each almost to the edge. Top with the cheese and sprinkle with the oregano. Brush the edge of each round with a little water and fold over the uncovered sides. Press the edges to seal.

Bake for about 15 minutes, until golden and crisp. Remove from the oven and leave to stand for 2 minutes, then transfer to warmed plates and serve.

serves 2–4

2 tbsp olive oil, plus extra for brushing

1 quantity Pizza Dough (see page 95), or 1 x 25-cm/ 10-inch pizza base

plain flour, for dusting

1 quantity basic Tomato Sauce (see page 91)

70 g/2^1/$_2$ oz cooked, peeled prawns

55 g/2 oz artichoke hearts, thinly sliced

25 g/1 oz mozzarella cheese, drained and thinly sliced

1 tomato, thinly sliced

100 g/3^1/$_2$ oz mushrooms or pepperoni, thinly sliced

2 tsp capers, rinsed

2 tsp stoned, black olives

salt and pepper

four seasons pizza

Preheat the oven to 220°C/400°F/Gas Mark 6 and brush a baking sheet with olive oil.

Roll out the dough on a lightly floured surface to a 25-cm/ 10-inch round. Place on the baking sheet and push up the edge a little. Cover and let stand in a warm place for 10 minutes.

Spread the Tomato Sauce over the pizza base, almost to the edge. Cover one quarter with prawns. Cover a second quarter with artichoke hearts. Cover the third quarter with alternate slices of mozzarella and tomato. Cover the final quarter with the sliced mushrooms. Sprinkle the whole surface with capers and olives, season to taste with salt and pepper, and drizzle with the olive oil.

Bake in the oven for 20–25 minutes, until the crust is crisp and the cheese has melted. Serve immediately.

makes two 23-cm/9-inch pizzas

olive oil, for brushing

1 quantity Pizza Dough (see page 95)

2 courgettes

300 g/10½ oz buffalo mozzarella

1½–2 tbsp finely chopped fresh rosemary, or ½ tbsp dried rosemary

pizza bianca

Preheat the oven to 220°C/425°F/Gas Mark 7. Brush a baking sheet with oil.

Divide the dough in half and shape each half into a ball. Cover 1 ball and roll out the other into a 23-cm/9-inch round. Place the round on a lightly floured baking sheet.

Meanwhile, using a vegetable peeler, cut long, thin strips of courgette. Drain and dice the mozzarella.

Scatter half the mozzarella over the base. Add half of the courgette strips and sprinkle with half of the rosemary. Repeat with the remaining dough and topping ingredients.

Bake the two pizzas in the preheated oven for 15 minutes or until crispy. Serve immediately.

serves 2–4

olive oil, for brushing

1 quantity Pizza Dough
(see page 95), or 1 x 25-cm/
10-inch pizza base

plain flour, for dusting

25 g/1 oz fresh parsley,
chopped

25 g/1 oz fresh basil, chopped

15 g/$^{1}/_{2}$ oz fresh chives,
chopped

15 g/$^{1}/_{2}$ oz fresh marjoram,
chopped

2 garlic cloves, finely
chopped

125 ml/4 fl oz sour cream

1 tbsp olive oil flavoured with
mixed herbs

115 g/4 oz Parmesan cheese,
freshly grated

salt and pepper

mixed herbs pizza

Preheat the oven to 200°C/400°F/Gas Mark 6. Brush a baking
sheet with oil.

Roll out the dough on a lightly floured surface to a 25-cm/
10-inch round. Place on the baking sheet and push up the edge a
little. Cover and leave to stand in a warm place for 10 minutes.

Mix together the parsley, basil, chives, marjoram, garlic and sour
cream in a bowl and season with salt and pepper. Brush the pizza
base with the flavoured oil, then spread the herb mixture evenly
over it almost to the edge. Sprinkle with the Parmesan and bake
for 20 minutes, until crisp and golden. Serve immediately.

serves 2–4

6 tbsp olive oil, plus extra for brushing

300 g/10½ oz onions, halved and thinly sliced

50 ml/2 fl oz dry white wine

1 tbsp white wine vinegar

1 tsp lemon juice

1 quantity Pizza Dough (see page 95), or 1 x 25-cm/10-inch pizza base

plain flour, for dusting

225 g/8 oz mozzarella cheese, diced

2 tbsp chopped fresh parsley

salt and pepper

for the rocket pesto

70 g/2½ oz rocket, chopped

2 tbsp pine kernels

2 garlic cloves, chopped

30 g/1¼ oz Parmesan cheese, freshly grated

caramelized onion & rocket pesto pizza

Heat 2 tablespoons of the oil in a heavy-based saucepan. Add the onions, cover and cook over a very low heat, stirring occasionally, for 1 hour. Increase the heat to medium, uncover the pan and cook until all the liquid has evaporated and the onions are golden brown. Stir in the wine, vinegar and lemon juice, season with salt and pepper and cook, stirring constantly, until the liquid has almost evaporated. Remove the pan from the heat.

Meanwhile, pound the rocket, pine kernels and garlic to a paste with a pestle and mortar. Gradually beat in the oil, then stir in the Parmesan. Alternatively, use a food processor or blender. Season with salt and pepper.

Preheat the oven to 200°C/400°F/Gas Mark 6. Brush a baking sheet with oil. Roll out the dough on a lightly floured surface to a 25-cm/10-inch round. Place on the baking sheet and push up the edge a little. Cover and leave to stand in a warm place for 10 minutes.

Spread the rocket pesto evenly over the pizza base almost to the edge, then do the same with the caramelized onions. Sprinkle with the mozzarella and then with the parsley. Drizzle with the remaining olive oil and bake for 20 minutes, until crisp and golden. Serve immediately.

makes 10

1 quantity Pizza Dough
(see page 95)

plain flour, for dusting

1 quantity basic Tomato
Sauce (see page 91)

85 g/3 oz mozzarella cheese,
diced

85 g/3 oz sliced ham, salami
or smoked chicken, cut into
strips

2 fresh marjoram sprigs,
chopped

1 litre/1¾ pints groundnut
oil

deep-fried pizza sandwiches

Divide the dough into 10 pieces and roll out each piece to a round on a lightly floured surface.

Spread the Tomato Sauce evenly over the rounds, leaving a 2-cm/¾-inch margin around the edges. Divide the cheese, meat and marjoram between the rounds. Brush the margins of the rounds with water, fold over the dough and press the edges firmly to seal.

Heat the oil in a deep-fryer or heavy-based saucepan to 180–190°C/350–375°F or until a cube of bread browns in 30 seconds. Add the pizza sandwiches, in batches, and cook for 10 minutes, until crisp and golden brown. Drain well on kitchen paper and keep warm while cooking the remaining batches. Serve hot.

serves 2–4

3 tbsp olive oil

1 onion, chopped

2 garlic cloves, chopped

70 g/2^1/$_2$ oz mushrooms, sliced

1 quantity Pizza Dough (see page 95)

plain flour, for dusting

200 g/7 oz canned sweetcorn, drained

200 g/7 oz canned chopped tomatoes

115 g/4 oz pepperoni sausage, sliced

55 g/2 oz Cheddar cheese, grated

pinch of dried oregano

salt and pepper

upside-down pizza

Preheat the oven to 200°C/400°F/Gas Mark 6.

Heat 2 tbsp of the oil in a 25-cm/10-inch frying pan. Add the onion and cook over a low heat, stirring occasionally, for 5 minutes. Add the garlic and mushrooms and cook, stirring occasionally, for 5 minutes more. Remove the pan from the heat, drain off the oil and leave to cool.

Roll out the dough on a lightly floured surface to a 25-cm/10-inch round. Cover and leave to stand in a warm place for 10 minutes.

Stir the sweetcorn, tomatoes, pepperoni, cheese and oregano into the onion mixture (still in the frying pan) and season with salt and pepper. Place the dough round on top of the filling and tuck in the edge all the way round. Prick a few small holes in the dough to allow steam to escape during cooking and brush with the remaining olive oil. Bake for 18–20 minutes. (If the handle of your frying pan will not withstand the heat of the oven, transfer the mixture to a 25-cm/10-inch round baking tin before adding the dough.)

To serve, place a plate on top of the pizza and, holding the pan and plate firmly together, invert the two. Lift off the pan and serve the pizza immediately.

serves 2–4

olive oil, for brushing

1 quantity Pizza Dough
(see page 95), or 1 x 25-cm/
10-inch pizza base

plain flour for dusting

2 plum tomatoes, diced

2 shallots, diced

175 g/6 oz salmon fillet,
skinned and diced

salt and pepper

for the tzatziki

200 ml/7 fl oz Greek-style
yogurt

4 spring onions, finely
chopped

1 mini cucumber, diced

1 garlic clove, finely chopped

2 tbsp chopped fresh mint

salmon & tzatziki pizza

Preheat the oven to 200°C/400°F/Gas Mark 6. Brush a baking sheet with oil.

Roll out the dough on a lightly floured surface to a 25-cm/ 10-inch round. Place on the baking sheet and push up the edge a little. Cover and leave to stand in a warm place for 10 minutes.

Sprinkle the tomatoes and shallots evenly over the pizza base almost to the edge. Top with the salmon and season with salt and pepper. Bake for 20 minutes, until crisp and golden.

Meanwhile, make the tzatziki. Lightly whisk the yogurt with a fork in a bowl. Stir in the spring onions, cucumber, garlic and mint and season with salt and pepper.

Remove the pizza from the oven and top with a little of the tzatziki. Serve immediately with the remaining tzatziki.

serves 2–4

olive oil, for brushing

1 fresh red chilli

200 ml/7 fl oz canned coconut milk

1 tbsp red curry paste

1 tbsp soft dark brown sugar

1 tbsp Thai fish sauce

1 lemon grass stalk, lightly crushed

175 g/6 oz skinless boneless chicken breast portion, cut into strips

25 g/1 oz roasted peanuts, ground

1 quantity Pizza Dough (see page 95), or 1 x 25-cm/ 10-inch pizza base

plain flour, for dusting

salt and pepper

fresh basil leaves, to garnish

Thai curry pizza

Preheat the oven to 200°C/400°F/Gas Mark 6. Brush a baking sheet with oil.

Deseed the chilli if you prefer a milder flavour and slice thinly. Heat half the coconut milk in a heavy-based saucepan. Stir in the curry paste and cook, stirring, until it gives off its aroma. Add the sugar, fish sauce and lemon grass and cook, stirring constantly, until the mixture is a rich golden brown colour.

Add the remaining coconut milk and bring back to the boil, then stir in the chicken, peanuts and chilli. Lower the heat and simmer for 10–15 minutes, until most of the liquid has evaporated.

Roll out the dough on a lightly floured surface to a 25-cm/ 10-inch round. Place on the baking sheet and push up the edge a little. Cover and leave to stand in a warm place for 10 minutes.

Remove the pan from the heat. Remove and discard the lemon grass and season the curry to taste with salt and pepper. Spoon the curry on to the pizza base, spreading it out almost to the edge. Bake for 20 minutes, until crisp and golden, and serve immediately, garnished with basil leaves.

Wraps

The wrap is the new take on our old favourite, the sandwich. Wraps are light, bright, fun and healthy – great for packed lunches, light lunches, relaxed outdoor eating or an informal dinner party with friends.

Wraps are big business these days and although they seem to have appeared from nowhere, the wrap has a history of its own. Bobby Valentine, an American former baseball manager, is credited with the invention of the wrap sandwich at his Connecticut restaurant.

Variety

Wraps are one food that will satisfy both healthy eaters and those looking for a guilty pleasure. Whether you're dieting or not, wraps are definitely on the menu. They are easy to prepare and good for the whole family. They take just a few minutes to put together and so are ideal for packed lunches. Variations in tortilla ingredients cater for all needs; for more fibre, substitute whole wheat tortillas for your normal wraps. Or for wheat-free recipes, try corn tortillas instead.

Evening entertaining

Wrap and tortilla-based meals are perfect for a casual evening with friends. Mediterranean-inspired recipes are ideal for *al fresco* eating. You can offer several different wraps to accommodate vegetarians and meat-eaters with the minimum of fuss. With an array of fresh ingredients and bright colours, wraps look delicious and take little or no cooking. No wonder they are so popular!

Appetizers and desserts

Wraps are even great to serve as appetizers or desserts. Why not try a modern twist on the traditional appetizers with a Prawn & Avocado Wrap (see page 211)?

For those with a sweet tooth, crêpes and pancakes offer an easy and tasty dessert that can be whipped up in an instant, for example a simple Chocolate & Banana Pancake (see page 241).

Children's favourite
Children love wraps as they can eat them with their fingers. If you are worried about you or your children eating enough vegetables, then wraps are a great way to encourage a wider variety of greens on the menu. Half the fun with wraps is that you can really involve your children in the preparation of ingredients, plus the actual wrapping!

Wrapping – 'the roll'
This is the easiest way. Simply place your filling in the centre of the wrap and spread in a vertical line to the end of the top and bottom sides. Then either fold the left and right sides over the filling, or fold one side over the filling and roll the filled section over the other side. However, be careful not to drop the filling out of the ends of the wrap.

'Open ended'
This way you see the filling at one end but the other end is folded. This method is like creating a pocket. Place your filling in the centre of the tortilla and spread in a vertical line to the end of the top side. Fold the bottom third of the tortilla up over the filling. Take the left and right sides of the tortilla (the part that has no filling on it) and fold it over the filling creating an easy-to-eat pocket.

Don't forget to put out plenty of napkins for sticky fingers!

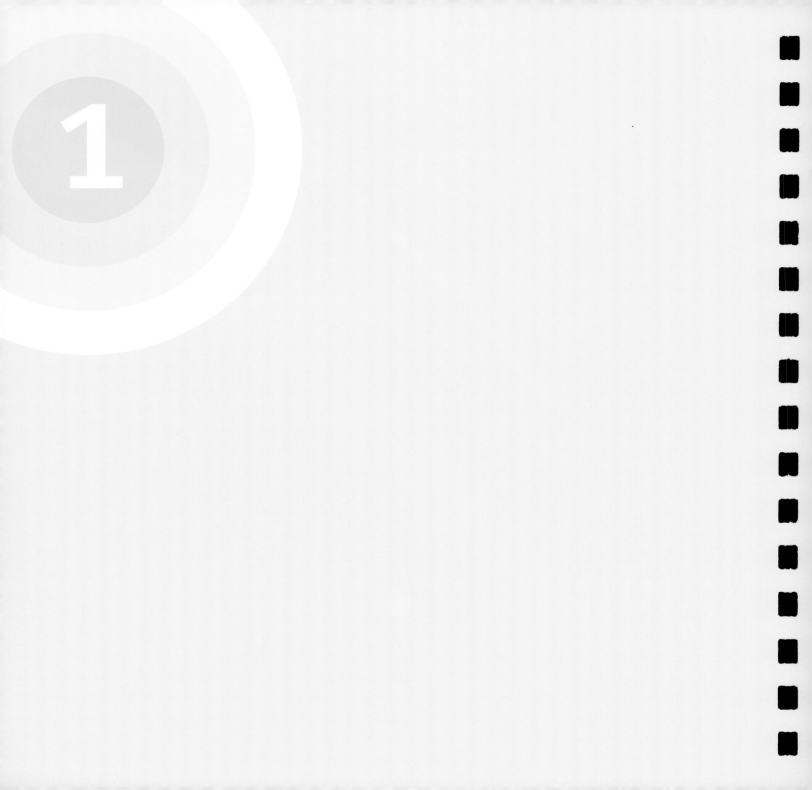

It's a Wrap!

makes 8

3 tbsp olive oil, plus extra for drizzling

3 tbsp maple syrup or clear honey

1 tbsp red wine vinegar

2 garlic cloves, crushed

2 tsp dried oregano

1–2 tsp dried red chilli flakes

4 chicken breasts, skinless and boneless

2 red peppers, deseeded and cut into 2.5-cm/1-inch strips

salt and pepper

8 tortillas, warmed, to serve

green salad and guacamole, to serve

chicken fajitas

Place the oil, maple syrup, vinegar, garlic, oregano, chilli flakes and salt and pepper to taste in a large, shallow dish or bowl and mix together.

Slice the chicken across the grain into slices 2.5 cm/1 inch thick. Toss in the marinade until well coated. Cover and leave to chill in the refrigerator for 2–3 hours, turning occasionally.

Heat a griddle pan until hot. Lift the chicken slices from the marinade with a slotted spoon, lay on the griddle pan and cook over a medium–high heat for 3–4 minutes on each side, or until cooked through. Remove the chicken to a warmed serving plate and keep warm.

Add the peppers to the griddle pan, skin side down, and cook for 2 minutes on each side. Transfer to the serving plate.

Serve immediately with the warmed wraps, a green salad and guacamole.

makes 4

2 medium-sized chicken
breasts

1 tbsp olive oil

2 eggs

4 x 25-cm/10-inch sun-dried
tomato wraps

4 baby gem lettuce leaves,
washed

4 white anchovies

20 g/¾ oz freshly grated
Parmesan cheese

salt and pepper

for the caesar dressing

3 tbsp mayonnaise

1 tbsp water

½ tbsp white wine vinegar

salt and pepper

caesar chicken wraps

Preheat oven to 200°C/400°F/Gas Mark 6.

Place the chicken breasts on a non-stick baking tray; rub with the olive oil and season with salt and pepper. Bake in the oven for 20 minutes. Remove and leave to cool.

Bring a small saucepan of water to the boil, add the eggs, and cook for 9 minutes, then cool under cold running water for 5 minutes. Once cooled, peel and roughly chop the eggs. Shred the chicken and combine with the chopped eggs.

To make the dressing, put the mayonnaise, water, white wine vinegar and salt and pepper to taste in a screw-top jar and shake until blended. Combine with the chicken and egg and set aside.

Preheat a non-stick pan or grill pan until almost smoking, then cook the wraps one at a time for 10 seconds on each side. This will add some colour and also soften the wraps.

Place a lettuce leaf in the middle of each wrap, top with the chicken, eggs, anchovies and Parmesan, then roll up. Cut into slices and serve.

makes 4

4 x 25-cm/10-inch wraps

55 g/2 oz cranberry sauce

255 g/9 oz cooked turkey
breast, shredded

150 g/5¹/₂ oz brie, sliced

salt and pepper

turkey wraps with brie & cranberry

Preheat a non-stick pan or grill pan until almost smoking, then cook the wraps one at a time for 10 seconds on each side. This will add some colour and also soften the wraps.

Spread the cranberry sauce over the wraps and divide the turkey and brie between the wraps, placing in the middle of each wrap. Sprinkle with salt and pepper and then fold at the ends. Roll up, cut in half on an angle and serve.

makes 8

2 tbsp olive oil, plus extra for
oiling

2 large onions, thinly sliced

550 g/1 lb 4 oz lean beef,
cut into bite-size pieces

1 tbsp ground cumin

1–2 tsp cayenne pepper,
or to taste

1 tsp paprika

8 soft corn tortillas

1 quantity of bottled
Taco Sauce, warmed and
thinned with a little water if
necessary

225 g/8 oz Cheddar cheese,
grated

salt and pepper

to serve

avocado, diced

red onion, finely chopped

mustard

beef enchiladas

Preheat the oven to 180°C/350°F/Gas Mark 4. Oil a large,
rectangular baking dish.

Heat the oil in a large frying pan over a low heat. Add the onions
and cook for 10 minutes, or until soft and golden. Remove with a
slotted spoon and reserve.

Increase the heat to high, add the beef and cook, stirring, for
2–3 minutes, or until browned on all sides. Reduce the heat to
medium, add the spices and salt and pepper to taste and cook,
stirring constantly, for 2 minutes.

Warm each tortilla in a lightly oiled non-stick frying pan for
15 seconds on each side, then dip each, in turn, in the sauce. Top
with a little of the beef, onions and grated cheese and roll up.

Place seam side down in the prepared baking dish, top with
the remaining sauce and grated cheese and bake in the
preheated oven for 30 minutes. Serve with the avocado, red
onion and mustard.

makes 4

250 g/9 oz sirloin steak

1 tbsp olive oil

1 tbsp mayonnaise

125 g/4^1/$_2$ oz Stilton cheese, crumbled

4 x 25-cm/10-inch wraps

^{1}/$_2$ small bag watercress

salt and pepper

beef & stilton wraps

Season the steak with salt and pepper.

Preheat a non-stick pan till almost smoking. Add the oil, and then seal the steak, cooking for 30 seconds on each side. Remove from the pan and set aside for a few minutes. Once the steak has rested, cut into thin strips with a sharp knife.

Mix together the mayonnaise and Stilton cheese.

Preheat a non-stick pan or grill pan until almost smoking, then cook the wraps one at a time for 10 seconds on each side. This will add some colour and also soften the wraps.

Divide the steak between the wraps, placing along the middle of each wrap. Top with the Stilton and mayonnaise, and then finish with watercress. Roll up, cut in half and serve.

makes 4

2 rump steaks, about 225 g/8 oz each

finely grated rind and juice of 1 lime

1 fresh green chilli, seeded and finely chopped

2 garlic cloves, crushed

4 wheat tortillas

tomato salsa and soured cream, to serve

for the marinade

pinch of sugar

2 tbsp olive oil

1 small onion, thinly sliced

1 red pepper, thinly sliced

salt and pepper

steak & lime tortillas

Thinly slice the steaks. To make the marinade, put the lime rind and juice, chilli, garlic, sugar, and salt and pepper to taste into a large, shallow, non-metallic dish and mix together. Add the steak and turn in the marinade to coat it. Cover and let marinate in the refrigerator for 3–4 hours, turning occasionally.

Heat the oil in a large frying pan over medium heat. Add the onion and red pepper and cook, stirring frequently, for 5 minutes until softened. Using a slotted spoon, remove the steak from the marinade, add to the frying pan, and cook, stirring constantly, for 2–3 minutes until browned. Add the marinade, bring to the boil, and toss together.

Meanwhile, warm the tortillas according to the instructions on the package. Divide the steak mixture among the tortillas, then fold in one side and roll up each tortilla to form an open-ended pocket. Serve hot with tomato salsa and soured cream to spoon on top.

makes 4

½ duck

85 g/3 oz rhubarb

1 tbsp water

2 tsp white sugar

4 x 25-cm/10-inch multigrain wraps

1 mango, peeled and sliced

4 spring onions, cut into 5-cm/2-inch pieces

small bunch of coriander

salt and pepper

crispy duck wraps with mango & rhubarb

Preheat oven 220°C/425°F/Gas Mark 7.

Place the duck in the oven on a non-stick baking tray and cook for 20–25 minutes or until crispy. Remove from the oven and leave in a warm place to cool.

In a small pan heat the rhubarb with 1 tbsp of water and the sugar, and cook for about 5 minutes or until the rhubarb starts to soften. Remove the pan from the heat and leave to cool.

Pull all the meat off the duck and shred.

Preheat a non-stick pan or grill pan until almost smoking, then cook the wraps one at a time on both sides for 10 seconds. This will add some colour and also soften the wraps.

Divide the duck, mango and spring onions between the wraps, placing along the middle of each wrap. Sprinkle with salt and pepper, top with a spoonful of rhubarb and coriander and then roll up, cut in half on an angle and serve.

makes 4

310 g/11 oz lamb leg steak

¹/2 tbsp olive oil

4 x 25-cm/10-inch wraps

100 g /3¹/2 oz canned piquillo
peppers, drained and sliced

55 g/2 oz stoned green olives

small bunch of fresh
flat-leaf parsley

salt and pepper

for the aïoli

3 tbsp mayonnaise

1 tbsp extra virgin olive oil

1 clove garlic, crushed

salt and pepper

lamb wraps with peppers & aïoli

Rub the lamb with olive oil, salt and pepper.

Preheat a grill pan until almost smoking. Cook the lamb for
2–3 minutes on each side. The lamb should be pink in the
middle. Remove and set aside in a warm place.

To make the aïoli, mix together the mayonnaise, olive oil and
garlic and season with salt and pepper.

Slice the lamb into thin strips.

Preheat a non-stick pan or grill pan until almost smoking, then
cook the wraps one at a time for 10 seconds on each side. This
will add some colour and also soften the wraps.

Divide the lamb between the wraps, placing along the middle.

Top with the peppers, olives and parsley and spoon over the
aïoli. Roll up and serve.

makes 4

2 tsp mustard

55 g/2 oz chunky apple sauce

4 x 25-cm/10-inch wraps

280 g/10 oz roast pork, shredded

100 g/3$\frac{1}{2}$ oz mature Cheddar cheese, sliced

salt and pepper

roast pork wraps with apple & cheddar

Mix together the mustard and apple sauce and season with salt and pepper.

Preheat a non-stick pan or grill pan until almost smoking, then cook the wraps one at a time for 10 seconds on each side. This will add some colour and also soften the wraps.

Divide the roast pork and Cheddar cheese between the wraps, placing in the middle of each wrap. Top with the mustard and apple sauce mixture and then fold at the ends. Roll up, cut in half and serve.

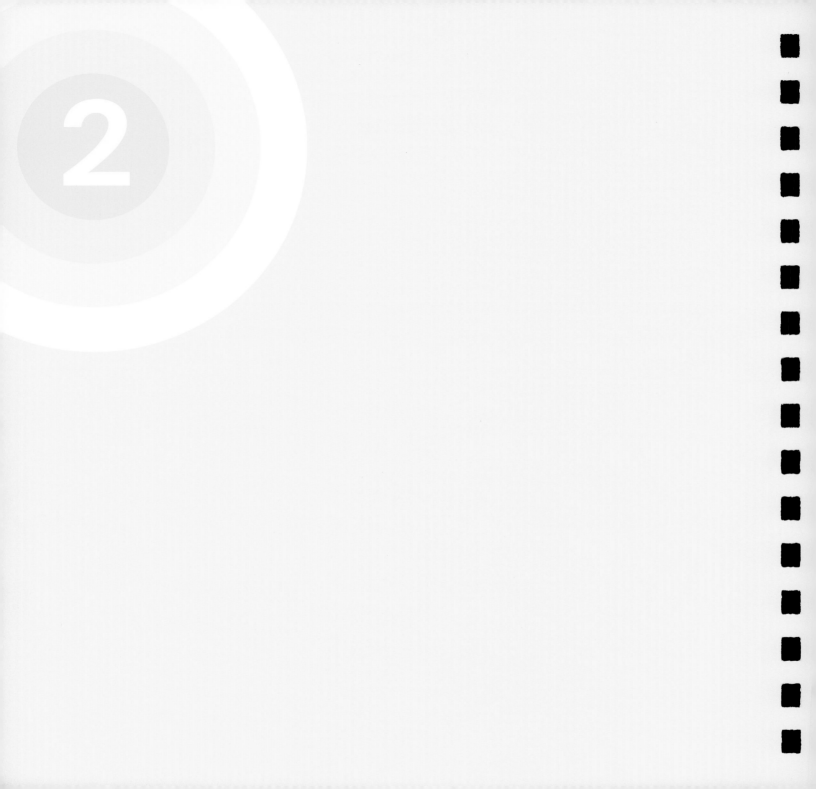

Fisherman's Catch

makes 4

310 g/11 oz fresh salmon
fillet

1 tbsp olive oil

4 eggs

2 tbsp mayonnaise

2 tbsp soured cream

20 g/3/4 oz capers, chopped

zest of 1 lemon

chopped fresh dill

4 x 25-cm/10-inch wraps

salt and pepper

salmon & dill wraps

Preheat oven 200°C/400°F/Gas Mark 6.

Place the salmon on a non-stick baking tray, brush with olive oil and season with salt and pepper. Cook in the oven for 8–10 minutes. Remove and leave to cool.

Bring a small saucepan of water to the boil, add the eggs, and cook for 9 minutes, then cool under cold running water for 5 minutes. Once cooled, peel and roughly chop the eggs.

Flake the salmon into a bowl, removing the skin if there is any. Add the eggs, mayonnaise, soured cream, capers, lemon zest and dill.

Preheat a non-stick pan or grill pan until almost smoking, then cook the wraps one at a time for 10 seconds on each side. This will add some colour and also soften the wraps.

Divide the salmon mixture between the wraps, placing in the middle of each wrap. Then fold at the ends, roll up, cut in half and serve.

makes 4

4 x 25-cm/10-inch wraps

200 g/7 oz cooked crayfish tails

1 mango, peeled and sliced

½ cucumber, deseeded and quartered

small bunch of fresh mint

small bunch of fresh coriander

for the dressing

2 tbsp yogurt

1 tbsp mayonnaise

1 tsp medium curry paste

1 tsp mango chutney

salt and pepper

crayfish wraps with mango & cucumber

To make the dressing, mix together all the ingredients.

Preheat a non-stick pan or grill pan until almost smoking, then cook the wraps one at a time for 10 seconds on each side. This will add some colour and also soften the wraps.

Divide the crayfish between the wraps, placing them in the middle of each wrap, and then top with mango, cucumber, mint and coriander.

Spoon over the dressing, then fold the wraps in at the ends, roll up, cut into slices and serve.

makes 4

200 g/7 oz tinned tuna, drained

4 tbsp mayonnaise

70 g/2½ oz pitted green olives, chopped

4 spring onions, sliced

small bunch of fresh flat-leaf parsley, shredded

4 lettuce leaves, washed

4 x 25-cm/10-inch wraps

salt and pepper

tuna mayonnaise wraps with olives

Mix together the tuna, mayonnaise, olives, spring onions and parsley in a bowl, then season with salt and pepper.

Preheat a non-stick pan or grill pan until almost smoking, then cook the wraps one at a time for 10 seconds on each side. This will add some colour and also soften the wraps.

Place a lettuce leaf in the middle of each wrap, then divide the tuna mixture between the wraps, placing on top of the lettuce leaf. Fold at the ends, roll up, cut into slices and serve.

makes 4

250 g/9 oz baby fennel

150 g/5½ oz fresh or canned
white crabmeat

4 tbsp mayonnaise

zest and juice of 1 lemon

small bunch of fresh
flat-leaf parsley, shredded

4 x 25-cm/10-inch
Mediterranean herb wraps

salt and pepper

crab & fennel wraps

Cut the fennel in half lengthways and then slice thinly.

Place the sliced fennel in a bowl with the crabmeat, mayonnaise, salt and pepper, lemon zest and juice and the parsley. Mix well.

Leave for 5 minutes to allow the lemon juice to wilt the fennel slightly.

Preheat a non-stick pan or grill pan until almost smoking, then cook the wraps one at a time for 10 seconds on each side. This will add some colour and also soften the wraps.

Give the filling mixture another stir and then divide between the wraps, placing in the middle of each wrap. Then fold at the ends, roll up, cut in half on an angle and serve.

makes 8

about 450 g/1 lb firm-fleshed white fish, such as red snapper or cod

¼ tsp ground cumin

pinch of dried oregano

4 garlic cloves, very finely chopped

150 ml/5 fl oz fish stock

juice of ½ lemon or lime

8 flour tortillas

2–3 romaine lettuce leaves, shredded

2 ripe tomatoes, diced

salt and pepper

salsa, to serve

lemon halves, to garnish

fish burritos

Season the fish to taste with salt and pepper, then place in a pan with the cumin, oregano, garlic, and enough stock to cover.

Bring to the boil, then cook for 1 minute. Remove the pan from the heat. Let the fish cool in the cooking liquid for 30 minutes.

Remove the fish from the liquid with a slotted spoon and break up into bite-sized pieces. Place in a non-metallic bowl, sprinkle with the lemon juice, and set aside.

Heat the tortillas, one at a time, in a non-stick pan, sprinkling them with a few drops of water as they heat. Wrap the tortillas in foil or a clean tea towel to keep them warm while you heat up the rest.

Arrange the shredded lettuce in the middle of one tortilla, spoon on a few big chunks of the fish, then sprinkle with the tomatoes, add some salsa and roll up. Repeat with the other tortillas. Serve immediately, garnished with lemon halves.

makes 4

½ cucumber

200 g/7 oz smoked mackerel, flaked

200 g/7 oz cream cheese

½ red onion, finely chopped

1 tbsp horseradish

zest of 1 lemon

chopped fresh dill

pepper

4 x 25-cm/10-inch wraps

smoked mackerel wraps with horseradish

Cut the cucumber in half, scrape out the seeds with a spoon and then cut into small dice.

Place the cucumber, mackerel, cream cheese, onion and horseradish in a bowl and mix well. Once combined add the lemon zest, dill and pepper. You will not need salt, as the mackerel is salty enough.

Preheat a non-stick pan or grill pan until almost smoking, then cook the wraps one at a time for 10 seconds on each side. This will add some colour and also soften the wraps.

Divide the mackerel mixture between the wraps, spreading the mixture evenly over the wrap. Fold in half and then again and again. You should end up with a cone-shaped wrap.

makes 4

310 g/11 oz fresh tuna steak

1 tbsp olive oil

½ tsp cracked black pepper

½ tsp cumin seeds

4 x 25-cm/10-inch sun-dried tomato wraps

salt

for the tabbouli

20 g/¾ oz couscous

1 tbsp extra virgin olive oil

1 tomato, chopped

1 spring onion, finely chopped

small bunch of fresh flat-leaf parsley, shredded

salt and pepper

tuna & tabbouli wraps

Rub the tuna in the olive oil, and sprinkle with the cracked black pepper, cumin and salt.

Heat a non-stick grill pan until almost smoking then grill the tuna for 30 seconds on each side. Remove from the pan and set aside. If you prefer your tuna more cooked through, cook it for another 30 seconds each side.

To make the tabbouli, put the couscous and olive oil in a heat-proof bowl, pour on enough hot water to just cover the couscous and leave for 5 minutes.

After 5 minutes stir the couscous with a fork to separate the grains. If the couscous is still a little hard add more water and repeat the process.

Add the tomato, spring onion and parsley to the couscous and season with salt and pepper to taste.

Preheat a non-stick pan or grill pan until almost smoking, then cook the wraps one at a time for 10 seconds on each side. This will add some colour and also soften the wraps.

Divide the tabbouli between the wraps and top with the tuna pieces, then fold at the ends, roll up and serve.

makes 4

1 ripe avocado

200 g/7 oz cooked peeled prawns

4 x 25-cm/10-inch wraps

4 baby gem lettuce leaves

for the dressing

3 tbsp mayonnaise

1 tbsp tomato ketchup

1 tsp Worcestershire sauce

dash of Tabasco

salt and pepper

prawn & avocado wraps

Cut the avocado in half, remove the skin and stone and cut each half into four pieces.

To make the dressing, mix together the mayonnaise, tomato ketchup, Worcestershire sauce and Tabasco, in a bowl. Season with salt and pepper, add the prawns and mix again.

Preheat a non-stick pan or grill pan until almost smoking, then cook the wraps one at a time for 10 seconds on each side. This will add some colour and also soften the wraps.

Place a lettuce leaf in the middle of each wrap and divide the prawn mixture between the wraps. Top with avocado, and then fold in at the ends. Roll up, cut in half and serve.

3

Fresh from the Garden

makes 8

25 g/1 oz unsalted butter

¹/₂ tbsp sunflower oil

200 g/7 oz leeks, halved, rinsed and finely shredded

freshly grated nutmeg, to taste

1 tbsp finely snipped fresh chives

8 savoury crêpes

85 g/3 oz soft goat's cheese, rind removed if necessary, chopped

salt and pepper

leek & goat's cheese crêpes

Melt the butter with the oil in a heavy-based saucepan with a lid over a medium–high heat. Add the leeks and stir around so that they are well coated. Stir in salt and pepper to taste, but remember the cheese might be salty. Add a few gratings of nutmeg, then cover the leeks with a sheet of wet greaseproof paper and put the lid on the saucepan. Reduce the heat to very low and leave the leeks to sweat for 5–7 minutes until very tender, but not brown. Stir in the chives, then taste and adjust the seasoning if necessary.

Place 1 crêpe on the work surface and put one-eighth of the leeks on the crêpe, top with one-eighth of the cheese, then fold the crêpe into a square parcel or simply roll it around the filling. Continue to fill and fold or roll the remaining crêpes.

Should you wish to serve the crêpes hot, preheat the oven to 200°C/400°F/Gas Mark 6. Place the crêpes on a baking tray in the oven and bake for 5 minutes, or until the crêpes are hot and the cheese starts to melt.

makes 4

1 red onion, cut into eighths

1 red pepper, cored and
cut into eighths

1 small aubergine,
cut into eighths

1 courgette, cut into eighths

4 tbsp extra virgin olive oil

1 clove of garlic, crushed

100 g/3$\frac{1}{2}$ oz feta cheese,
crumbled

small bunch of fresh mint,
shredded

4 x 25-cm/10-inch sun-dried
tomato wraps

salt and pepper

roasted vegetable & feta cheese wraps

Preheat the oven to 220°C/425°F/Gas Mark 7.

Mix together all the vegetables, olive oil, garlic, salt and pepper and place in the oven in a non-stick oven tray. Roast for 15–20 minutes or until golden and cooked through.

Remove from the oven and leave to cool. Once cool, mix in the feta and mint.

Preheat a non-stick pan or grill pan until almost smoking, then cook the wraps one at a time on both sides for 10 seconds. This will add some colour and also soften the wraps.

Divide the vegetable and feta mixture between the wraps, placing along the middle of each wrap, roll up, cut in half and serve.

serves 4

2 tbsp olive oil

1 large onion, finely chopped

225 g/8 oz button mushrooms, finely sliced

2 fresh mild green chillies, seeded and finely chopped

2 garlic cloves, crushed

250 g/9 oz spinach leaves, torn into pieces if large

175 g/6 oz Cheddar cheese, grated

8 flour tortillas

vegetable oil, for deep-frying

spinach & mushroom chimichangas

Heat the oil in a large, heavy-based frying pan. Add the onion and cook over a medium heat for 5 minutes, or until softened.

Add the mushrooms, chillies and garlic and cook for 5 minutes, or until the mushrooms are lightly browned. Add the spinach and cook, stirring, for 1–2 minutes, or until just wilted. Add the cheese and stir until just melted.

Spoon an equal quantity of the mixture into the centre of each tortilla. Fold in 2 opposite sides of each tortilla to cover the filling, then roll up to enclose it completely.

Heat the oil for deep-frying in a deep-fryer or large, deep saucepan to 180–190°C/350–375°F, or until a cube of bread browns in 30 seconds. Deep-fry the chimichangas 2 at a time, turning once, for 5–6 minutes, or until crisp and golden. Drain on kitchen paper before serving.

makes 4

4 x 25-cm/10-inch wraps

4 cherry tomatoes, halved

1/2 cucumber, deseeded and quartered

55 g/2 oz baby spinach leaves

for the hummus

200 g/7 oz canned chickpeas, drained

1 clove garlic, crushed

4 tbsp extra virgin olive oil

1 tsp tahini

1 tsp lemon juice

55 g/2 oz stoned green olives, chopped

small bunch of flat-leaf parsley, shredded

salt and pepper

green olive hummus wraps

To make the hummus place the chickpeas, garlic, olive oil, tahini and lemon juice in a food processor and blend until smooth. Season with salt and pepper. Scrape into a bowl and mix in the olives and parsley.

Preheat a non-stick pan or grill pan until almost smoking, then cook the wraps one at a time for 10 seconds on each side. This will add some colour and also soften the wraps.

Spread the hummus over the wraps and divide the cherry tomatoes, cucumber and spinach between them, placing in the middle of each wrap. Fold at the ends, roll up, cut in half and serve.

makes 4

100 g/3½ oz green beans, trimmed

100 g/3½ oz canned borlotti beans, drained

100 g/3½ oz canned red kidney beans, drained

½ red onion, finely sliced

4 tbsp extra virgin olive oil

1 tsp red wine vinegar

100 g/3½ oz cooked beetroot

1 ripe avocado

4 x 25-cm/10-inch herb wraps

salt and pepper

three-bean wraps

Blanch the green beans in salted, boiling water for 30 seconds and then run under a cold tap until cold. Drain and reserve.

Place the borlotti beans, kidney beans, red onion, olive oil and red wine vinegar in a bowl, add the green beans and season with salt and pepper.

Meanwhile cut the beetroot into 2.5-cm/1-inch dice and cut the avocado in half and remove the stone. Peel and roughly chop, before adding to the bean mixture with the diced beetroot. Mix well.

Preheat a non-stick pan or grill pan until almost smoking, then cook the wraps one at a time for 10 seconds on each side. This will add some colour and also soften the wraps.

Divide the filling between the wraps, placing in the middle of each wrap, and then fold at the ends. Roll up, cut in half and serve.

makes 4

280 g/10 oz cooked beetroot, diced

100 g/3^{1}/$_{2}$ oz Roquefort cheese, crumbled

100 g/3^{1}/$_{2}$ oz walnuts, halved

1 tbsp mayonnaise

55 g/2 oz rocket

4 x 25-cm/10-inch multigrain wraps

pepper

beet & roquefort wraps

Mix together the beetroot, Roquefort, walnuts, and mayonnaise. Season with pepper to taste and gently add the rocket leaves.

Preheat a non-stick pan or grill pan until almost smoking, then cook the wraps one at a time for 10 seconds on each side. This will add some colour and also soften the wraps.

Divide the mixture between the wraps, placing in the middle of each wrap, and then fold at the ends. Roll up, cut in half and serve.

makes 4

3 red onions, cut into eighths

3 tbsp extra virgin olive oil

250 g/9 oz goat's cheese, crumbled

100 g/3^{1}/$_{2}$ oz toasted flaked almonds

1–2 tbsp shredded fresh flat-leaf parsley

4 x 25-cm/10-inch wraps

salt and pepper

goat's cheese & caramelized onion wraps

Preheat the oven to 220°C/425°F/Gas Mark 7.

Mix together the onions and olive oil and season with salt and pepper. Place on a non-stick oven tray, and cook in the oven for 15–20 minutes until golden and cooked through.

Remove from the oven and leave to cool.

Combine the onion mixture with the goat's cheese, almonds and parsley and set aside.

Preheat a non-stick pan or grill pan until almost smoking, then cook the wraps one at a time for 10 seconds on each side. This will add some colour and also soften the wraps.

Divide the filling between the wraps, spreading the mixture evenly over the wrap. Fold in half and then again and again. You should end up with a nice cone-shaped wrap. Serve immediately.

makes 4

200 g/7 oz new potatoes,
halved

4 eggs

55 g/2 oz watercress

4 tbsp mayonnaise

1 tsp mustard

1 small white onion,
finely chopped

4 x 25-cm/10-inch wraps

salt and pepper

egg & watercress wraps

Put the new potatoes in a small pan and cover with water, add a small amount of salt. Bring to the boil and then simmer for 15 minutes or until cooked. Drain and, once cool, chop the potatoes into bite–sized pieces.

Bring a small saucepan of water to the boil, add the eggs and cook for 9 minutes, then cool under running water for 5 minutes. Once cooled, peel and reserve.

Roughly chop the watercress and eggs and then place in a bowl with the potatoes, mayonnaise, mustard and onion. Season with salt and pepper, then mix until all the ingredients are well combined.

Preheat a non-stick pan or grill pan until almost smoking, then cook the wraps one at a time for 10 seconds on each side. This will add some colour and also soften the wraps.

Divide the mixture between the wraps, placing in the middle of each wrap, and then fold at the ends. Roll up, cut in half and serve.

makes 4

4 x 25-cm/10-inch wraps

3 fresh buffalo mozzarella cheeses, drained and sliced

4 plum tomatoes, each one cut into eighths

55 g/2 oz rocket

for the pesto

70 g/2½ oz pine nuts

1 clove garlic, crushed

1 small bunch basil

4 tbsp extra virgin olive oil

70 g/2½ oz Parmesan cheese, freshly grated

salt and pepper

mozzarella & pesto wraps

To make the pesto put the pine nuts, garlic and basil in a food processor, then blend, adding the olive oil a tablespoon at a time. When the mixture is smooth, scrape into a bowl, and add the Parmesan cheese and the salt and pepper.

Preheat a non-stick pan or grill pan until almost smoking, then cook the wraps one at a time for 10 seconds on each side. This will add some colour and also soften the wraps.

Spread the pesto over the wraps.

Divide the slices of mozzarella between the wraps. Place in the middle of each wrap, top with the plum tomatoes and rocket. Fold at the ends. Roll up, then cut into slices and serve.

All Things
Sweet

makes 8–10

115 g/4 oz plain flour

25 g/1 oz cocoa powder

pinch of salt

1 egg

25 g/1 oz caster sugar

350 ml/12 fl oz milk

50 g/1¾ oz butter

icing sugar, for dusting

ice cream or pouring cream,
to serve

for the berry compote

150 g/5½ oz fresh
blackberries

150 g/5½ oz fresh blueberries

225 g/8 oz fresh raspberries

55 g/2 oz caster sugar

juice of ½ lemon

½ tsp mixed spice (optional)

chocolate crêpes with berry compote

Preheat the oven to 140°C/275°F/Gas Mark 1. Sift together the flour, cocoa powder and salt into a large bowl and make a well in the centre.

Beat together the egg, sugar and half the milk in a separate bowl, then pour into the dry ingredients. Beat together, until a smooth batter is formed. Gradually beat in the remaining milk. Pour the batter into a jug.

Heat an 18-cm/7-inch non-stick frying pan over a medium heat and add 1 teaspoon of the butter.

When the butter has melted, pour in enough batter to cover the bottom, then swirl it around the pan so that you have a thin layer. Cook for 30 seconds and then lift the crêpe to check it is cooked. Loosen the edges of the crêpe, then flip it over. Cook on the other side until the base is golden brown.

Transfer the crêpe to a warmed plate and keep warm in the preheated oven while you cook the remaining batter, adding the remaining butter to the frying pan as necessary. Make a stack of the crêpes with baking paper in between each one.

To make the compote, pick over the berries and put in a saucepan with the sugar, lemon juice and mixed spice, if using. Cook over a low heat until the sugar has dissolved and the berries are warmed through. Do not overcook.

Put a crêpe on a warmed serving plate and spoon some of the compote on to the centre. Either roll or fold the crêpe and dust with icing sugar. Repeat with the remaining crêpes. Serve with ice cream or pouring cream.

crêpes suzette

makes 8

8 sweet crêpes made with the finely grated rind of 1 lemon added to the batter

2 tbsp brandy

for the orange sauce

55 g/2 oz caster sugar

1 tbsp water

finely grated rind of 1 large orange

125 ml/4 fl oz freshly squeezed orange juice

55 g/2 oz unsalted butter, diced

1 tbsp Cointreau, Grand Marnier or other orange-flavoured liqueur

To make the orange sauce, place the sugar in a wide sauté or frying pan over a medium heat and stir in the water. Continue stirring until the sugar dissolves, then increase the heat to high and leave the syrup to bubble for 1–2 minutes until it just begins to turn golden brown.

Stir in the orange rind and juice, then add the butter and continue stirring until it melts. Stir in the orange-flavoured liqueur.

Lay one of the crêpes flat in the sauté pan and spoon the sauce over. Using a fork and the spoon, fold the crêpe into quarters and push to the side of the pan. Add the next crêpe to the pan and repeat. Continue until all the crêpes are coated with the sauce and folded. Remove the pan from the heat.

Warm the brandy in a ladle or small saucepan, ignite and pour it over the crêpes to flambé, shaking the sauté pan.

When the flames die down, serve the crêpes with the sauce spooned over.

makes 4

1 large mango, peeled and cut into large pieces

1 small pineapple, peeled cored and cut into large chunks

4 tbsp Greek yogurt

1 tbsp honey

4 x 25-cm/10-inch plain wraps

4 tbsp honey

1 tsp allspice

sweet & spicy wraps

Preheat the grill to high.

Mix together the mango, pineapple, yogurt and honey.

Brush the wraps with honey, sprinkle with allspice and place under the grill for 1 minute. This will add some colour and soften the wraps.

Divide the fruit mixture between the wraps, placing down the middle. Roll up and serve.

makes 8

3 large bananas

6 tbsp orange juice

grated rind of 1 orange

2 tbsp orange- or banana-
flavoured liqueur

for the hot chocolate sauce

1 tbsp cocoa powder

2 tsp cornflour

3 tbsp milk

40 g/1½ oz plain chocolate,
broken into pieces

1 tbsp butter

175 g/6 oz golden syrup

¼ tsp vanilla essence

for the pancakes

115 g/4 oz plain flour

1 tbsp cocoa powder

1 egg

1 tsp sunflower oil

300 ml/10 fl oz milk

oil, for frying

chocolate & banana pancakes

Peel and slice the bananas and arrange them in a dish with the orange juice and rind and the liqueur. Set aside.

To make the sauce, mix the cocoa and cornflour in a bowl, then stir in the milk. Put the chocolate in a saucepan with the butter and golden syrup. Heat gently, stirring until well blended. Add the cocoa mixture and bring to the boil over gentle heat, stirring. Simmer for 1 minute, then remove from the heat and stir in the vanilla essence.

To make the pancakes, sift the flour and cocoa into a mixing bowl and make a well in the centre. Add the egg and oil. Gradually whisk in the milk to form a smooth batter. Heat a little oil in a heavy-based frying pan and pour off any excess. Pour in a little batter and tilt the frying pan to coat the base. Cook over medium heat until the underside is browned. Flip over and cook the other side. Slide the pancake out of the frying pan and keep warm. Repeat until all the batter has been used.

To serve, reheat the chocolate sauce for 1–2 minutes. Fill the pancakes with the bananas and fold in half or into triangles. Pour over a little chocolate sauce and serve.

makes 8

for the pancakes

150 g/5¹/2 oz plain flour

pinch of salt

1 egg

1 egg yolk

300 ml/10 fl oz coconut milk

4 tsp vegetable oil,
plus extra for frying

for the filling

1 banana

1 papaya

juice of 1 lime

2 passion fruit

1 mango, peeled, stoned and
sliced

4 lychees, stoned and halved

1–2 tbsp honey

flowers or fresh mint sprigs,
to decorate

exotic fruit pancakes

Sift the flour and salt into a bowl. Make a well in the centre and add the egg, egg yolk and a little of the coconut milk. Gradually draw the flour into the egg mixture, beating well and gradually adding the remaining coconut milk to form a smooth batter. Stir in the oil. Cover and chill for 30 minutes.

Peel and slice the banana and place in a bowl. Peel and slice the papaya, discarding the seeds. Add to the banana with the lime juice and mix well. Cut the passion fruit in half and scoop out the flesh and seeds into the fruit bowl. Stir in the mango, lychees and honey.

Heat a little oil in a 15-cm/6-inch frying pan. Pour in just enough of the batter to cover the base of the frying pan and tilt so that it spreads thinly and evenly. Cook until the pancake is just set and the underside is lightly browned, turn and briefly cook the other side. Remove from the frying pan and keep warm. Repeat with the remaining batter to make a total of 8 pancakes.

To serve, place a little of the prepared fruit filling along the centre of each pancake and then roll it into a cone shape. Lay on warmed serving plates, decorate with flowers or mint sprigs and serve.

makes 4

300 g/10½ oz apples, peeled
and cored

55 g/2oz sultanas

2 tbsp soft brown sugar

1 tsp cinnamon

4 x sheets filo pastry

4 tbsp butter, melted

icing sugar, for dusting

warm filo wraps with spiced apples

Preheat the oven 200°C/400°C/Gas Mark 6. Cut the apples
into 2.5-cm/1-inch pieces, mix with the sultanas, sugar and
cinnamon.

Lay the filo pastry sheets out and brush with melted butter. Fold
each one in half and brush once more with butter.

Divide the apple mixture between the filo pastry sheets, placing
in the middle of one end. Fold over each side and roll into a
cylinder shape. Brush with butter and dust with icing sugar.

Place in the oven on a non-stick baking tray for 10 minutes or
until golden.

Divide between 4 warmed plates and serve.

makes 4

½ tbsp vegetable oil

55 g/2 oz blanched almonds

15 g/½ oz pistachios

150 g/5 oz honey

100 g/3½ oz stale breadcrumbs

zest of ½ orange

4 x round sheets Asian rice paper

rice paper wraps with pistachios & almonds

Heat the oil in a frying pan and fry the almonds until they start to colour, then add the pistachios. Remove from the pan when the nuts are golden.

Heat the honey in a saucepan over a low heat; add the nuts, breadcrumbs and the orange zest.

Stir continually for 5 minutes until the mixture has thickened to a paste. Remove from the heat and leave to cool.

Place the rice papers on a flat surface and brush with warm water, they will soften and become pliable after a few minutes.

Divide the nut mixture between the rice papers, placing in the middle in a cylinder shape. Fold over at the ends, roll up carefully and serve.

makes 4

100 g/3½ oz dried figs,
chopped

100 g/3½ oz dried dates,
chopped

15 g/½ oz stem ginger in
syrup, chopped

20 g/¾ oz ginger syrup

200 g/7 oz sushi rice

1¼ cups water

1 tbsp rice vinegar

1 tbsp sugar

sweet sushi wraps

In a large bowl, mix together the dried figs and dates, the stem ginger and the ginger syrup. Leave to infuse for 10 minutes.

Wash the rice in a sieve under a cold running tap until the water runs clear.

Add the water to the rice in a non-stick heavy-based saucepan, bring to the boil and then turn down the heat to low, cook with a lid on until all of the water has disappeared. This will take about 6 minutes. Remove from the heat and leave to sit for 15 minutes.

Stir the vinegar and sugar into the rice.

Place a sushi mat on a flat surface and cover with a layer of clingfilm.

Using wet fingers, place half of the rice on the mat, spreading it out evenly, until it covers the mat.

Place half of the filling along the centre of the rice.

Lift up the edge of the mat closest to you, and slowly roll away from you in a smooth movement until you have formed a cylinder shape, applying gentle pressure to keep it neat and compact.

Repeat the process with the remaining rice and filling.

Cut off the ends and cut in half and serve.

makes 4

200 g/7 oz dried apricots

150 g/5½ oz rhubarb,
roughly chopped

½ pint/300 ml water

70 g/2½ oz sugar

icing sugar, for dusting

whipped cream, to serve

for the calzone

225 g/8 oz plain flour,
plus extra for dusting

½ tsp salt

½ tsp easy-blend dried yeast

90 ml/3 fl oz milk

50 ml/2 fl oz tepid water

1 tsp olive oil, plus extra for
brushing

sweet filled calzone with apricots & rhubarb

Place the dried apricots, rhubarb, water and sugar in a heavy-based saucepan and stew over a low heat for 15–20 minutes. Remove and leave to cool.

To make the calzone, sift the flour and salt into a bowl; add the yeast, milk and water. Mix with your hands until well combined, turn out onto a floured surface and knead for 5 minutes or until silky. Using your fingers, make indentations in the dough and pour over the olive oil. Mix thoroughly until all of the oil has been absorbed.

Shape the dough into a ball and place in a clean bowl, brush with oil, then cover with clingfilm. Leave at room temperature for 1–1½ hours or until the mixture has doubled in size.

Preheat the oven to its highest setting, then place a heavy non-stick baking sheet inside.

Divide the dough into 4 on a floured surface and roll into thin circles. Divide the filling between the circles, placing in the middle. Brush with water and fold over, pinching at the edges. Dust with icing sugar. Remove the tray from the oven, carefully place on the calzone and bake for 8–10 minutes or until golden. Serve with whipped cream.

Bite-size

A morsel of something delicious and tantalizing is all you need to make the perfect party. Bite-size entertaining is well and truly back in vogue. For gourmet menus with the minimum of effort, try the fabulous collection of recipe ideas in this chapter.

Bite-size dining is great for any occasion and can be as chic or as informal as you want. Forget stuffy seating plans and masses of silver cutlery – this season it's all about getting fun and friendly. You could host an early evening cocktail party accompanied by a light and delicious buffet, or turn a drinks party into a real occasion with a really sumptuous spread.

Don't be daunted by making your own canapés. They are easy to prepare in advance, look fantastic and are sure to create a good impression. For maximum impact nibbles should emphasize visual style as well as taste; colour, shape and texture are all important. From traditional and much-loved classics to more modern and exotic creations, this chapter provides a palette of flavours from across the globe.

Choosing the menu

Setting the menu is crucial in determining the mood and feel of your gathering. Think about the evening's occasion, the season and the guests' requirements. For a luxurious cocktail party, pick the most impressive-looking dishes. If you are hosting a small and intimate gathering then you may focus the menu on your friends' favourite foods. For a summer soirée, you may decide to plan vegetable and seafood dishes for *al fresco* eating. Think about what vegetables are in season and shop no earlier than the day before the party to ensure you get the freshest ingredients. Most importantly, your menu should contain a variety of

colours, textures and shapes. Don't forget to ask any vegetarian, gluten-free or dairy-free diners to give you prior warning of special requirements.

Preparation
Once you have chosen an array of delicacies you can plan your strategy. Make a list of ingredients and shop the day before. It is important to prepare what you can in advance and refrigerate. This will leave you with time to organize the house and plan your outfit with plenty of time to spare. Make sure you work in an organized space; clean down work surfaces between each dish and wash up as you go to maintain a calm and serene kitchen. You can always ask friends to prepare a specific bite and give them the recipe in advance.

Presentation
Presentation is the key to producing a breathtaking spread. Serving platters and bowls should be attractive, spotless and matching. You may want to theme the crockery; for example, try chic Japanese platters or colourful Mediterranean dishes. You could include different-shaped plates and bowls, or serve food on wooden boards. All white or all black dishes can be quite striking, and they provide a simple canvas for the attractive nibbles.

If you aren't able to match the crockery then try lining dishes with simple but effective napkins; that way a theme is maintained without a matching set. Keep garnishes to a minimum so as not to distract from the food. Small, practical details can make the difference between a messy eating experience and a sophisticated party. Provide small glasses for used skewers, several finger bowls with lemons and plenty of attractive napkins.

Canapés

makes 20

plain flour, for dusting

200 g/7 oz ready-made puff
pastry, thawed if frozen

3 tbsp pesto

20 cherry tomatoes, each cut
into 3 slices

115 g/4 oz goat's cheese

salt and pepper

fresh basil sprigs, to garnish

pesto & goat's cheese tartlets

Preheat the oven to 200°C/400°F/Gas Mark 6, then lightly flour a baking sheet. Roll out the pastry on a floured work surface to 3 mm/⅛ inch thick. Cut out 20 rounds with a 5-cm/2-inch plain cutter and arrange the pastry rounds on the floured baking sheet.

Spread a little pesto on each round, leaving a margin around the edge, then arrange 3 tomato slices on top of each one.

Crumble the goat's cheese over and season to taste with salt and pepper. Bake in the preheated oven for 10 minutes, or until the pastry is puffed up, crisp and golden. Garnish with basil sprigs and serve warm.

makes 32

2 tbsp extra virgin olive oil,
plus extra for brushing and
drizzling

1 onion, finely chopped

1 garlic clove, finely chopped

400 g/14 oz canned chopped
tomatoes

125 g/4 1/2 oz baby spinach
leaves

25 g/1 oz pine nuts

salt and pepper

for the bread dough

100 ml/3 1/2 fl oz warm water

1/2 tsp easy-blend dried yeast

pinch of sugar

200 g/7 oz strong white flour,
plus extra for dusting

1/2 tsp salt

spanish spinach & tomato pizzas

To make the bread dough, measure the water into a small bowl, sprinkle in the dried yeast and sugar and leave in a warm place for 10–15 minutes, or until frothy.

Meanwhile, sift the flour and salt into a large bowl. Make a well in the centre of the flour and pour in the yeast liquid, then mix together with a wooden spoon. Using your hands, work the mixture until it leaves the sides of the bowl clean.

Turn the dough out on to a lightly floured work surface and knead for 10 minutes, or until smooth and elastic and no longer sticky. Shape into a ball and put it in a clean bowl. Cover with a clean, damp tea towel and leave in a warm place for 1 hour, or until it has risen and doubled in size.

To make the topping, heat the oil in a large, heavy-based frying pan. Add the onion and cook for 5 minutes, or until soft. Add the garlic and cook for 30 seconds. Stir in the tomatoes and cook for 5 minutes, stirring occasionally, until reduced to a thick mixture. Add the spinach leaves and cook, stirring, until wilted. Season to taste with salt and pepper.

While the dough is rising, preheat the oven to 200°C/400°F/Gas Mark 6. Brush several baking trays with olive oil. Turn the dough out on to a lightly floured work surface and knead well for 2–3 minutes to knock out the air bubbles. Roll out the dough very thinly and, using a 6-cm/2 1/2-inch plain, round cutter, cut out 32 rounds. Place on the prepared baking sheets.

Spread each base with the spinach mixture, sprinkle over the pine nuts and drizzle with a little of the olive oil. Bake in the oven for 10–15 minutes, or until the edges are golden.

makes 8

1 small French baguette

4 tomatoes, thinly sliced

4 hard-boiled eggs

4 bottled or canned anchovy fillets in olive oil, drained and halved lengthways

8 marinated, stoned black olives

for the tapenade

100 g/3¹/2 oz stoned black olives

6 bottled or canned anchovy fillets in olive oil, drained

2 tbsp capers, rinsed

2 garlic cloves, roughly chopped

1 tsp Dijon mustard

2 tbsp lemon juice

1 tsp fresh thyme leaves

4–5 tbsp olive oil

pepper

egg & tapenade toasts

To make the tapenade, place the olives, anchovies, capers, garlic, mustard, lemon juice, thyme and pepper to taste in a food processor and process for 20–25 seconds, or until smooth. Scrape down the sides of the mixing bowl. With the motor running, gradually add the oil through the feeder tube to make a smooth paste. Spoon the paste into a bowl, cover with clingfilm and set aside until required.

Preheat the grill to medium. Cut the French baguette into 8 slices, discarding the crusty ends. Toast on both sides under the hot grill until light golden brown. Leave to cool.

To assemble the toasts, spread a little of the tapenade on 1 side of each slice of toast. Top with the tomato slices. Peel the hard-boiled eggs, then slice and arrange over the tomatoes. Dot each egg slice with a little of the remaining tapenade and top with anchovies. Halve the marinated olives and arrange 2 halves on each toast. Serve immediately.

makes 24

4 spring onions, white parts and half the green parts, very finely chopped

1/2 lemon, sliced

1 bay leaf, torn in half

1/2 tsp black peppercorns, lightly crushed

125 ml/4 fl oz dry white wine

450 g/1 lb boneless salmon, cut into pieces

115 g/4 oz butter, at room temperature

140 g/5 oz smoked salmon, cut into pieces

1/4 tsp ground nutmeg

2 tbsp very finely chopped fresh parsley

salt and pepper

12 large slices country-style bread, such as sourdough, each about 1 cm/1/2 inch thick

smoked salmon pâté

Put the onions, lemon slices, bay leaf, peppercorns and white wine in a large frying pan, add water to half-fill the pan and bring to the boil. Boil for 2 minutes, and then reduce the heat to its lowest setting. Add the salmon pieces, cover the pan and leave to simmer for 8 minutes. Remove the pan from the heat, keep covered and allow the salmon to cool in the cooking liquid.

Meanwhile, melt 25 g/1 oz of the butter in a large frying pan over a medium heat. Add the smoked salmon pieces and nutmeg and stir for about 2 minutes, until the salmon loses its shiny coral colour and becomes opaque. Remove from the heat and set aside until cool.

Drain and flake the poached salmon and put into a wide, shallow bowl. Add the smoked salmon mixture, cooking juices and the remaining butter and use your fingers to mix it all together until the salmon is very finely mixed. Stir in the parsley. Taste and adjust the seasoning, although you probably won't need much salt because of the flavour of the smoked salmon. Spoon into a bowl, cover and chill until 30 minutes before you are ready to serve.

When you are ready to serve, preheat the grill to high. Toast the bread on both sides until golden brown and crisp, then cut each slice in half. Spread the salmon pâté on the hot toast and serve.

serves 4

2 tbsp butter, melted, plus extra for greasing

225 g/8 oz waxy potatoes, finely diced

500 g/1 lb 2 oz fresh baby spinach

2 tbsp water

1 tomato, deseeded and chopped

1/4 tsp chilli powder

1/2 tsp lemon juice

225 g/8 oz (8 sheets) filo pastry, thawed if frozen

salt and pepper

potato & spinach triangles

Preheat the oven to 190°C/375°F/Gas Mark 5. Lightly grease a baking tray with a little butter. Cook the potatoes in a saucepan of lightly salted boiling water for 10 minutes, or until tender. Drain thoroughly and place in a mixing bowl.

Meanwhile, put the spinach into a large saucepan with the water, cover and cook, stirring occasionally, over a low heat for 2 minutes, or until wilted. Drain the spinach thoroughly, squeezing out the excess moisture, and add to the potatoes. Stir in the tomato, chilli powder and lemon juice. Season to taste with salt and pepper.

Lightly brush the sheets of filo pastry with melted butter. Spread out 4 of the sheets and lay a second sheet on top of each. Cut them into rectangles about 20 x 10 cm/8 x 4 inches.

Spoon a portion of the potato and spinach mixture onto one end of each rectangle. Fold a corner of the pastry over the filling, fold the pointed end back over the pastry strip, then fold over the remaining pastry to form a triangle.

Place the triangles on the prepared baking tray and bake in the preheated oven for 20 minutes, or until golden brown. Serve hot or cold.

makes 20

1 thin French baguette,
cut into 20 slices

*for the gorgonzola &
caramelized onion topping*

2 large onions, thinly sliced

25 g/1 oz butter

40 g/1½ oz caster sugar

225 ml/8 fl oz water

175 g/6 oz gorgonzola cheese

*for the tomato, avocado &
bacon topping*

55 g/2 oz chopped bacon

1 tbsp olive oil

1 large tomato, cored,
deseeded and finely diced

1–2 tbsp lemon juice

1–2 tbsp extra virgin olive oil

2 tbsp finely shredded basil
leaves

pinch of sugar

1 avocado

salt and pepper

topped crostini

Preheat the grill and place the bread slices on the grill rack
about 10 cm/4 inches from the source of the heat. Toast slowly
for 6–8 minutes, turning once, until crisp and golden on both
sides. Leave to cool.

To make the caramelized onions, put the onions, butter and half
the sugar in a saucepan with the water and bring to the boil.
Reduce the heat and simmer, uncovered, for about 20 minutes
until the onions are tender and the water has evaporated.
Transfer the onions to a frying pan, sprinkle with the remaining
sugar and stir over a medium–high heat until the sugar melts
and the onions are a light golden brown.

To make the tomato, avocado and bacon topping, put the
chopped bacon and olive oil in a frying pan over medium–high
heat and stir for about 5 minutes until the bacon is crisp.
Remove from the pan, drain on kitchen paper and then transfer
to a bowl. Add the tomato dice, lemon juice, olive oil, basil, sugar
and salt and pepper to taste and stir. Cut the avocado in half,
remove the stone and peel, then finely dice the flesh. Add to the
bowl and gently stir together, making sure the avocado is well
coated so it doesn't turn brown; add extra lemon juice or olive
oil, if necessary.

When ready to serve, cover 10 crostini with a small slice of
gorgonzola cheese, then top with a dollop of the caramelized
onions. Top the remaining crostini with the tomato, avocado and
bacon mixture. Arrange the crostini on large platters and serve.

makes 30

3 large potatoes, cut into chunks

85 g/3 oz frozen peas

55 g/2 oz frozen sweetcorn kernels, thawed

2 shallots, finely chopped

1 tsp ground cumin

1 tsp ground coriander

2 fresh green chillies, deseeded and finely chopped

2 tbsp chopped fresh mint

2 tbsp chopped fresh coriander

4 tbsp lemon juice

15 sheets filo pastry (about 12 x 18 cm/4^{1}/$_{2}$ x 7 inches), thawed if frozen

melted butter, for brushing

groundnut or sunflower oil, for deep-frying

salt

mango chutney, to serve

vegetable samosas

Place the potatoes in a saucepan and add cold water to cover and a pinch of salt. Bring to the boil, then reduce the heat, cover and simmer for 15–20 minutes, or until tender. Meanwhile, cook the peas according to the instructions on the packet, then drain. Drain the potatoes, return to the saucepan and mash coarsely with a potato masher or fork. Add the peas to the potatoes, then transfer to a bowl.

Add the sweetcorn, shallots, cumin, ground coriander, chillies, mint, fresh coriander and lemon juice and season to taste with salt. Mix well.

Keep the filo pastry sheets covered with clingfilm to prevent them from drying out. Take a sheet of filo pastry, brush with melted butter and cut in half lengthways. Place a tablespoonful of the filling in a corner of the pastry strip. Fold the pastry over at right angles to make a triangle, enclosing the filling. Continue folding in this way all the way down the strip to make a triangular parcel. Repeat with the remaining pastry sheets and filling.

Heat the oil in a deep-fat fryer or large saucepan to 180–190°C/350–375°F, or until a cube of bread browns in 30 seconds. Add the samosas, in batches, and cook until golden brown. Remove with a slotted spoon and drain on kitchen paper. Alternatively, bake the samosas in a preheated oven at 200°C/400°F/Gas Mark 6, for 10–15 minutes, or until golden brown. Serve the samosas hot or at room temperature with mango chutney.

makes 72

4 skinless, boneless chicken thighs

100 g/3¹/₂ oz cooked, peeled prawns

1 small egg, beaten

3 spring onions, finely chopped

2 garlic cloves, crushed

2 tbsp chopped fresh coriander

1 tbsp fish sauce

12 slices white bread, crusts removed

75 g/2³/₄ oz sesame seeds

sunflower oil, for frying

salt and pepper

shredded spring onion curls, to garnish

prawn & chicken sesame toasts

Place the chicken and prawns in a food processor and process until very finely chopped. Add the egg, spring onions, garlic, coriander, fish sauce and pepper and salt to taste and pulse for a few seconds to mix well. Transfer to a large bowl.

Spread the mixture evenly over the slices of bread, right to the edges. Sprinkle the sesame seeds onto a plate and press the chicken-and-prawn-topped side of each slice of bread into them to coat evenly.

Using a sharp knife, cut the bread into small squares, making 6 per slice.

Heat a 1-cm/¹/₂-inch depth of oil in a wide frying pan until very hot. Shallow-fry the bread rectangles quickly, in batches, for 2–3 minutes, or until golden brown all over, turning them over once.

Drain the toasts well on kitchen paper, transfer to a serving dish and garnish with shredded spring onion curls. Serve hot.

makes 12

100 g/4 oz puff pastry rolled
to a depth of 3mm/¹/8 inch

4 large fresh scallops,
cleaned and roe removed

extra virgin olive oil for
coating the scallops

salt and pepper

for the pea & mint purée

50 g/2 oz cooked peas

small clove garlic, grated

1 tbsp extra virgin olive oil

1 tbsp chopped mint

1 tbsp soured cream

1 tsp lemon juice

salt and pepper

mini tartlets with scallops & pea & mint purée

Preheat the oven to 180°C/ 350°F/Gas Mark 4. Using a 4-cm/
1½-inch round pastry cutter, cut out 12 pastry discs. Re-roll
and use the puff pastry leftovers if there is not enough to
make 12 discs.

Place the pastry discs on a flat tray, lined with greaseproof paper.
Lay another layer of greaseproof paper over the top and then
place a slightly smaller flat tray on top. (This will prevent the
puff pastry from rising in the oven.)

Leave the pastry to rest for 20 minutes in a cool place before
baking in the oven for 15–20 minutes or until golden. Remove
and leave to cool.

To make the pea and mint purée, blend the peas in a food
processor and add the garlic, extra virgin olive oil, mint, soured
cream, lemon juice, salt and pepper. Process until combined.
Scrape the mixture into a small container and place in the
refrigerator.

Heat a non-stick frying pan until just smoking. Toss the scallops
in a little extra virgin olive oil and season with salt and pepper.
Add the scallops to the pan and cook for 30 seconds each side.
Remove the scallops from the pan and set aside.

To assemble the canapés, place a small amount of pea and mint
purée on each mini tartlet. Cut each scallop into 3 slices and
arrange on top of the canapés. Serve immediately.

Elegant Nibbles

serves 6–8

4 large skinless, boneless chicken breasts

5 tbsp extra virgin olive oil

1 onion, finely chopped

6 garlic cloves, finely chopped

grated rind of 1 lemon, finely pared rind of 1 lemon and juice of both lemons

4 tbsp chopped fresh flat-leaf parsley

salt and pepper

lemon wedges and crusty bread, to serve

chicken in lemon & garlic

Using a sharp knife, slice the chicken breasts widthways into very thin slices. Heat the olive oil in a large, heavy-based frying pan, add the onion and fry for 5 minutes, or until softened but not browned. Add the garlic and fry for a further 30 seconds.

Add the sliced chicken to the pan and fry gently for 5–10 minutes, stirring from time to time, until all the ingredients are lightly browned and the chicken is tender.

Add the grated lemon rind and the lemon juice and let it bubble. At the same time, deglaze the pan by scraping and stirring all the bits on the base of the pan into the juices with a wooden spoon. Remove the pan from the heat, stir in the parsley and season to taste with salt and pepper.

Transfer the chicken in lemon and garlic, piping hot, to a warmed serving dish. Sprinkle with the pared lemon rind, and serve with lemon wedges for squeezing over the chicken, accompanied by chunks or slices of crusty bread for mopping up the lemon and garlic juices.

makes 12

350 g/12 oz monkfish tail or
250 g/9 oz monkfish fillet

12 stalks of fresh rosemary

3 tbsp extra virgin olive oil

juice of $1/2$ small lemon

1 garlic clove, crushed

salt and pepper

6 thick back bacon rashers

aïoli (see page 323), to serve

monkfish, rosemary & bacon skewers

If using monkfish tail, cut either side of the central bone with a sharp knife and remove the flesh to form 2 fillets. Slice the fillets in half lengthways, then cut each fillet into 12 bite-size chunks to give a total of 24 pieces. Put the monkfish pieces in a large bowl.

To prepare the rosemary skewers, strip the leaves off the stalks and reserve them, leaving a few leaves at one end.

For the marinade, finely chop the reserved leaves and whisk together in a bowl with the olive oil, lemon juice, garlic and salt and pepper to taste. Add the monkfish pieces and toss until coated in the marinade. Cover and leave to marinate in the refrigerator for 1–2 hours.

Preheat the grill to medium–high and arrange the skewers on the grill pan so that the leaves of the rosemary skewers protrude from the grill and therefore do not catch fire during cooking. Grill the monkfish and bacon skewers for 10 minutes, turning from time to time and basting with any remaining marinade, or until cooked. Serve hot accompanied by a bowl of aïoli in which to dip them.

makes 24

for the blinis

85 g/3 oz plain flour

1 tsp dried yeast

1/2 tsp sugar

150 ml/5 fl oz warm water

85 g/3 oz buckwheat flour

125 ml/4 fl oz warm milk

40 g/11/2 oz butter, melted
and cooled

1 large egg, separated

vegetable oil, for cooking

salt and pepper

for the topping

85 g/3 oz soured cream

finely grated rind of 2 lemons

55 g/2 oz smoked salmon,
very finely sliced

pepper

2 tbsp very finely snipped
chives, to garnish

smoked salmon blinis

To make the blinis, stir together the flour, yeast and sugar in a bowl. Make a well in the centre and slowly add the water, drawing in flour from the side to make a wet, lumpy batter. Beat until the batter is smooth, then stir in the buckwheat flour, cover the bowl tightly with a tea towel and set aside for 1 hour, until the batter has risen and the surface is covered with air bubbles.

Meanwhile, mix the soured cream with the lemon rind and pepper to taste. Cover and chill until ready to use. Stir together the milk, butter and egg yolk with a generous pinch of salt and pepper, then add to the batter, stirring well until blended. Beat the egg white in a separate bowl until peaks form, and then fold into the batter.

Heat a large frying pan over medium heat until you can feel the heat rising, then lightly brush the surface all over with vegetable oil using crumpled kitchen paper. Fill a tablespoon measure two-thirds full with the batter, then drop the batter on to the hot surface so it forms a circle about 5 cm/2 inches across; add as many more as will fit in the pan without touching. Cook for just over a minute, or until the top surface is covered with air holes and the bottom is golden brown and set. Use a palette knife to flip over the blinis and cook until set and golden brown. Transfer to a heatproof plate and keep warm in a low oven while you cook the remaining batter.

To serve, arrange the warm, not hot, blinis on a platter and top each with about 2 teaspoons of the chilled soured cream. Lay the salmon strips over the soured cream, add the snipped chives and serve.

makes 24

3 medium-sized heads chicory

115 g/4 oz blue cheese, such as Stilton, finely crumbled

4 tbsp pecan halves, very finely chopped

1 punnet mustard cress, to garnish

for the dressing

100 ml/3^1/$_2$ fl oz extra virgin olive oil

2^1/$_2$ tbsp balsamic vinegar

1 tsp Dijon mustard

1 tsp sugar

salt and pepper

pretty chicory bites

To make the dressing, put the oil, vinegar, mustard, sugar and salt and pepper to taste in a screw-top jar and shake until blended. Taste and adjust the seasoning, then set aside until required.

Cut the edges off the chicory heads so you can separate the leaves. Pick over the leaves and select the 24 best, boat-shaped leaves, then rinse them and pat dry.

Put the cheese and pecans in a bowl and gently toss together. Add 2 tablespoons of the dressing and toss again.

Arrange the chicory leaves on serving platters, then put a teaspoon of the cheese and pecans towards the pointed end of each leaf. Add small pieces of mustard cress to each to garnish. Cover and chill for up to an hour before serving.

serves 6

450 g/1 lb prepared squid

plain flour, for coating

sunflower oil, for deep-frying

salt

lemon wedges, to garnish

aïoli (see page 323), to serve

calamares

Slice the squid into 1-cm/½-inch rings and halve the tentacles if large. Rinse and dry well on kitchen paper so that they do not spit during cooking. Dust the squid rings with flour so that they are lightly coated.

Heat the sunflower oil in a deep fryer to 180–190°C/350–375°F, or until a cube of bread browns in 30 seconds. Carefully add the squid rings, in batches so that the temperature of the oil does not drop, and fry for 2–3 minutes, or until golden brown and crisp all over, turning several times. Do not overcook as the squid will become tough and rubbery rather than moist and tender.

Using a slotted spoon, remove the fried squid from the deep fryer and drain well on kitchen paper. Keep hot in a warm oven while you fry the remaining squid rings.

Sprinkle the fried squid rings with salt and serve piping hot, garnished with lemon wedges for squeezing over them. Accompany with a bowl of aïoli in which to dip the calamares.

serves 6–8

200 g/7 oz Manchego cheese

3 tbsp plain flour

1 egg

1 tsp water

85 g/3 oz fresh white or brown breadcrumbs

sunflower oil, for deep-frying

salt and pepper

fried manchego cheese

Slice the cheese into triangular shapes about 2 cm/¾ inch thick or alternatively into cubes measuring about the same size. Put the flour in a polythene bag and season with salt and pepper to taste. Break the egg into a shallow dish and beat together with the water. Spread the breadcrumbs on to a plate.

Toss the cheese pieces in the flour so that they are evenly coated, then dip the cheese in the egg mixture. Finally, dip the cheese in the breadcrumbs so that the pieces are coated on all sides. Transfer to a large plate and store in the refrigerator until you are ready to serve them.

Just before serving, heat about 2.5 cm/1 inch of the sunflower oil in a large, heavy-based frying pan or heat the oil in a deep fryer to 180–190°C/350–375°F, or until a cube of bread browns in 30 seconds. Add the cheese pieces, in batches of about 4 or 5 pieces so that the temperature of the oil does not drop, and fry for 1–2 minutes, turning once, until the cheese is just beginning to melt and they are golden brown on all sides. Do make sure that the oil is hot enough otherwise the coating on the cheese will take too long to become crisp and the cheese inside may ooze out.

Using a slotted spoon, remove the fried cheese from the frying pan or deep fryer and drain well on kitchen paper. Serve the fried cheese pieces hot, accompanied by cocktail sticks on which to spear them.

serves 8

800 g/1 lb 12 oz fresh mussels, in their shells

splash of dry white wine

1 bay leaf

85 g/3 oz butter

35 g/1¹⁄₄ oz fresh white or brown breadcrumbs

4 tbsp chopped fresh flat-leaf parsley, plus extra sprigs to garnish

2 tbsp snipped fresh chives

2 garlic cloves, finely chopped

salt and pepper

lemon wedges, to serve

mussels with herb & garlic butter

Clean the mussels by scrubbing or scraping the shells and pulling out any beards that are attached to them. Discard any with broken shells and any that refuse to close when tapped. Put the mussels in a colander and rinse well under cold running water. Preheat the oven to 230°C/450°F/Gas Mark 8.

Put the mussels in a large saucepan and add a splash of wine and the bay leaf. Cook, covered, over a high heat for 5 minutes, shaking the saucepan occasionally, or until the mussels are opened. Drain the mussels and discard any that remain closed.

Shell the mussels, reserving one half of each shell. Arrange the mussels, in their half shells, in a large, shallow, ovenproof serving dish.

Melt the butter and pour into a small bowl. Add the breadcrumbs, parsley, chives, garlic and salt and pepper to taste, and mix well together. Leave until the butter has set slightly. Using your fingers or 2 teaspoons, take a large pinch of the herb and butter mixture and use to fill each mussel shell, pressing it down well. Chill the filled mussels in the refrigerator until ready to serve.

To serve, bake the mussels in the oven for 10 minutes, or until hot. Serve immediately, garnished with parsley sprigs and accompanied by lemon wedges for squeezing over them.

makes 12

450 g/1 lb lean boneless pork

3 tbsp extra virgin olive oil,
plus extra for oiling (optional)

grated rind and juice of
1 large lemon

2 garlic cloves, crushed

2 tbsp chopped fresh flat-leaf
parsley, plus extra to garnish

1 tbsp ras-el-hanout spice
blend

salt and pepper

miniature pork brochettes

The brochettes are marinated overnight, so remember to do this in advance in order that they are ready when you need them. Cut the pork into pieces about 2 cm/¾ inch square and put in a large, shallow, non-metallic dish that will hold the pieces in a single layer.

To prepare the marinade, put all the remaining ingredients in a bowl and mix well together. Pour the marinade over the pork and toss the meat in it until well coated. Cover the dish and leave to marinate in the refrigerator for 8 hours or overnight, stirring the pork 2–3 times.

You can use wooden or metal skewers to cook the brochettes and for this recipe you will need 12 x 15-cm/6-inch skewers. If you are using wooden ones, soak them in cold water for about 30 minutes prior to using. This helps to stop them burning and the food sticking to them during cooking. Metal skewers simply need to be greased, and flat ones should be used in preference to round ones to prevent the food on them falling off.

Preheat the grill to medium–high. Thread about 3 marinated pork pieces, leaving a little space between each piece, on to each prepared skewer. Cook the brochettes for 10–15 minutes or until tender and lightly charred, turning several times and basting with the remaining marinade during cooking. Serve the pork brochettes piping hot, garnished with parsley.

serves 6

2 fresh tuna steaks, weighing about 250 g/9 oz in total and about 2.5 cm/1 inch thick

5 tbsp of extra virgin olive oil

3 tbsp red wine vinegar

4 sprigs of fresh thyme, plus extra to garnish

1 bay leaf

2 tbsp plain flour

1 onion, finely chopped

2 garlic cloves, finely chopped

85 g/3 oz pimiento-stuffed green olives, halved

salt and pepper

tuna with pimiento-stuffed olives

Don't get caught out with this recipe – the tuna steaks need to be marinated, so remember to start preparing the dish the day before you are going to serve it. Remove the skin from the tuna steaks, then cut the steaks in half along the grain of the fish. Cut each half into 1-cm/½-inch thick slices against the grain.

Put 3 tablespoons of the olive oil and the vinegar in a large, shallow, non-metallic dish. Strip the leaves from the sprigs of thyme and add these to the dish with the bay leaf and salt and pepper to taste. Add the prepared strips of tuna, cover the dish and leave to marinate in the refrigerator for 8 hours or overnight.

The next day, put the flour in a polythene bag. Remove the tuna strips from the marinade, reserving the marinade for later, add them to the bag of flour and toss well until they are lightly coated.

Heat the remaining olive oil in a large, heavy-based frying pan. Add the onion and garlic and gently fry for 5–10 minutes, or until softened and golden brown. Add the tuna strips to the pan and fry for 2–5 minutes, turning several times, until the fish becomes opaque. Add the reserved marinade and olives to the pan and cook for a further 1–2 minutes, stirring, until the fish is tender and the sauce has thickened.

Serve the tuna and olives piping hot, garnished with thyme sprigs.

Classic Bites

serves 4

125 ml/4 fl oz extra virgin olive oil

1 small oval-shaped loaf of white bread (ciabatta or bloomer), cut into 1-cm/ 1/2-inch slices

4 tomatoes, deseeded and diced

6 fresh basil leaves, torn, plus extra to garnish

8 black olives, stoned and chopped

1 large garlic clove, peeled and halved

salt and pepper

olive & tomato bruschetta

Pour half the oil into a shallow dish and place the bread in it. Leave for 1–2 minutes, then turn and leave for a further 2 minutes. The bread should be thoroughly saturated in the oil.

Meanwhile, put the tomatoes into a mixing bowl. Tear the basil leaves into pieces and sprinkle over the tomatoes. Season to taste with salt and pepper and add the olives. Pour over the remaining oil and leave to marinate while you toast the bruschetta.

Preheat the grill to medium. Place the bread on the grill rack and cook for 2 minutes on each side, or until golden and crisp.

Remove the bread from the grill and arrange on a plate.

Rub the cut edge of the garlic halves over the surface of the bruschetta, then top each slice with a spoonful of the tomato mixture. Serve immediately, garnished with basil leaves.

makes 16

1 potato, cut into chunks

pinch of salt

4 spring onions, chopped

1 garlic clove, chopped

1 tbsp chopped fresh thyme

1 tbsp chopped fresh basil

1 tbsp chopped fresh coriander

225 g/8 oz white crabmeat, drained if canned and thawed if frozen

1/2 tsp Dijon mustard

1/2 fresh green chilli, deseeded and finely chopped

1 egg, lightly beaten

plain flour, for dusting

sunflower oil, for frying

pepper

lime wedges, to garnish

dip or salsa of choice, to serve

crab cakes

Place the potato in a small saucepan and add water to cover. Add the salt. Bring to the boil, then reduce the heat, cover and simmer for 10–15 minutes, or until softened. Drain well, turn into a large bowl and mash with a potato masher or fork until smooth.

Meanwhile, place the spring onions, garlic, thyme, basil and coriander in a mortar and pound with a pestle until smooth. Add the herb paste to the mashed potato with the crabmeat, mustard, chilli, egg and pepper to taste. Mix well, cover with clingfilm and chill in the refrigerator for 30 minutes.

Sprinkle flour onto a shallow plate. Shape spoonfuls of the crabmeat mixture into small balls with your hands, then flatten slightly and dust with flour, shaking off any excess. Heat the oil in a frying pan over a high heat, add the crab cakes, in batches, and cook for 2–3 minutes on each side until golden. Remove from the pan and drain on kitchen paper. Set aside to cool to room temperature.

Arrange the crab cakes on a serving dish and garnish with lime wedges. Serve with a bowl of dip or salsa.

serves 6–8

55 g/2 oz white or brown bread, crusts removed

3 tbsp water

450 g/1 lb fresh lean pork mince

1 large onion, finely chopped

1 garlic clove, crushed

2 tbsp chopped fresh flat-leaf parsley, plus extra to garnish

1 egg, beaten

freshly grated nutmeg

flour, for coating

2 tbsp extra virgin olive oil

squeeze of lemon juice

salt and pepper

crusty bread, to serve

for the almond sauce

2 tbsp olive oil

25 g/1 oz white or brown bread

115 g/4 oz blanched almonds

2 garlic cloves, finely chopped

150 ml/5 fl oz dry white wine

425 ml/15 fl oz vegetable stock

salt and pepper

meatballs in almond sauce

To prepare the meatballs, put the bread in a bowl, add the water and soak for 5 minutes. With your hands, squeeze out the water and return the bread to the dried bowl. Add the pork, onion, garlic, parsley and egg, then season with nutmeg, and salt and pepper. Knead the ingredients together to form a smooth mixture.

Spread some flour on a plate. With floured hands, shape the meat mixture into about 30 equal-sized balls, then roll each meatball again in flour until coated.

Heat the olive oil in a large, heavy-based frying pan, add the meatballs, in batches so that they do not overcrowd the pan, and fry for 4–5 minutes, or until browned on all sides. Using a slotted spoon, remove the meatballs from the pan and set aside.

To make the almond sauce, heat the oil in the same frying pan in which the meatballs were cooked. Break the bread into pieces, add to the pan with the almonds and cook, stirring frequently, until the bread and almonds are golden. Add the garlic and cook for 30 seconds, then pour in the wine and boil for 1–2 minutes. Season to taste with salt and pepper and let cool.

Transfer the almond mixture to a food processor. Pour in the vegetable stock and blend the mixture until smooth. Return the sauce to the frying pan.

Carefully add the cooked meatballs to the sauce and simmer for 25 minutes, or until the meatballs are tender. Taste and season with salt and pepper if necessary. Transfer the cooked meatballs and sauce to a warmed serving dish, add a squeeze of lemon and garnish with chopped parsley. Serve hot accompanied by slices of crusty bread.

serves 12

350 g/12 oz long-grain rice

450 g/1 lb vine leaves, rinsed if preserved in brine

2 onions, finely chopped

1 bunch spring onions, finely chopped

1 bunch fresh parsley, finely chopped

25 g/1 oz fresh mint, finely chopped

1 tbsp fennel seeds

1 tsp crushed dried chillies

finely grated rind of 2 lemons

225 ml/8 fl oz extra virgin olive oil

600 ml/1 pint boiling water

salt

stuffed vine leaves

Bring a large saucepan of lightly salted water to the boil. Add the rice and return to the boil. Reduce the heat and simmer for 15 minutes, or until tender.

Meanwhile, if using preserved vine leaves, place them in a heatproof bowl and pour over boiling water to cover. Set aside to soak for 10 minutes. If using fresh vine leaves, bring a saucepan of water to the boil, add the vine leaves, then reduce the heat and simmer for 10 minutes.

Drain the rice and, while still hot, mix with the onions, spring onions, parsley, mint, fennel seeds, chillies, lemon rind and 3 tablespoons of the oil in a large bowl. Season to taste with salt.

Drain the vine leaves well. Spread out 1 leaf, vein side up, on a work surface. Place a generous teaspoonful of the rice mixture on the leaf near the stalk. Fold the stalk end over the filling, fold in the sides and roll up the leaf. Repeat until all the filling has been used. There may be some vine leaves left over – you can use them to line a serving platter, if wished.

Place the parcels in a large, heavy-based saucepan in a single layer (you may need to use 2 saucepans). Spoon over the remaining oil, then add the boiling water. Cover the parcels with an inverted heatproof plate to keep them below the surface of the water, cover the saucepan and simmer for 1 hour.

Allow the parcels to cool to room temperature in the saucepan, then transfer to a serving platter with a slotted spoon.

makes 40

55 g/2 oz canned anchovy fillets in olive oil, drained and roughly chopped

55 g/2 oz black olives, stoned and roughly chopped

115 g/4 oz Manchego or Cheddar cheese, finely grated

115 g/4 oz plain flour, plus extra for dusting

115 g/4 oz unsalted butter, diced

1/2 tsp cayenne pepper, plus extra for dusting

anchovy, olive & cheese triangles

Place the anchovies, olives, cheese, flour, butter and cayenne pepper in a food processor and pulse until a dough forms. Turn out and shape into a ball. Wrap in foil and chill in the refrigerator for 30 minutes.

Preheat the oven to 200°C/400°F/Gas Mark 6. Unwrap the dough, knead on a lightly floured work surface and roll out thinly. Using a sharp knife, cut it into strips about 5-cm/2-inches wide. Cut diagonally across each strip, turning the knife in alternate directions, to make triangles.

Arrange the triangles on 2 baking sheets and dust lightly with cayenne pepper. Bake in the preheated oven for 10 minutes, or until golden brown. Transfer to wire racks to cool completely.

makes 16

8 large eggs

2 whole pimientos (sweet red peppers) from a jar or can

8 green olives

5 tbsp mayonnaise

8 drops Tabasco sauce

large pinch cayenne pepper

salt and pepper

sprigs of fresh dill, to garnish

devilled eggs

To cook the eggs, put them in a saucepan, cover with cold water and slowly bring to the boil. Immediately reduce the heat to very low, cover and simmer gently for 10 minutes. As soon as the eggs are cooked, drain them and put under cold running water until they are cold. By doing this quickly, you will prevent a black ring from forming around the egg yolk. Gently tap the eggs to crack the eggshells and leave them until cold. When cold, crack the shells all over and remove them.

Using a stainless steel knife, halve the eggs lengthways, then carefully remove the yolks. Put the yolks in a nylon sieve, set over a bowl, and rub through, then mash them with a wooden spoon or fork. If necessary, rinse the egg whites under cold water and dry very carefully.

Put the pimientos on kitchen paper to dry well, then chop them finely, reserving a few strips. Finely chop the olives. If you are going to pipe the filling into the eggs, you need to chop both these ingredients very finely so that they will go through a 1-cm/½-inch nozzle. Add the chopped pimientos and most of the chopped olives to the mashed egg yolks, reserving 16 larger pieces for garnish. Add the mayonnaise, mix well together, then add the Tabasco sauce, cayenne pepper and salt and pepper to taste.

Using a piping bag with a 1-cm/½-inch nozzle, or a teaspoon, pipe or spoon the filling into each egg half. Arrange the eggs on a serving plate and add a small strip of the reserved pimientos and a piece of olive to the top of each stuffed egg. Garnish with dill sprigs and serve.

serves 8

450 g/1 lb can or jar unstoned
large green olives, drained

4 garlic cloves, peeled

2 tsp coriander seeds

1 small lemon

4 sprigs of fresh thyme

4 feathery stalks of fennel

2 small fresh red chillies
(optional)

extra virgin olive oil, to cover

pepper

cracked marinated olives

To allow the flavours of the marinade to penetrate the olives, place on a chopping board and, using a rolling pin, bash them lightly so that they crack slightly. Alternatively, use a sharp knife to cut a lengthways slit in each olive as far as the stone. Using the flat side of a broad knife, lightly crush each garlic clove. Using a pestle and mortar, crack the coriander seeds. Cut the lemon, with its rind, into small chunks.

Put the olives, garlic, coriander seeds, lemon chunks, thyme sprigs, fennel and chillies, if using, in a large bowl and toss together. Season with pepper to taste, but you should not need to add salt as conserved olives are usually salty enough. Pack the ingredients tightly into a glass jar with a lid. Pour in enough olive oil to cover the olives, then seal the jar tightly.

Leave the olives at room temperature for 24 hours, then marinate in the refrigerator for at least 1 week but preferably 2 weeks before serving. From time to time, gently give the jar a shake to re-mix the ingredients. Return the olives to room temperature and remove from the oil to serve. Provide cocktail sticks for spearing the olives.

serves 6

450 g/1 lb button mushrooms

5 tbsp olive oil

2 garlic cloves, finely chopped

squeeze of lemon juice

4 tbsp chopped fresh flat-leaf parsley

salt and pepper

crusty bread, to serve

sautéed garlic mushrooms

Wipe or brush clean the mushrooms, then trim off the stalks close to the caps. Cut any large mushrooms in half or into quarters. Heat the olive oil in a large, heavy-based frying pan, add the garlic and fry for 30 seconds–1 minute, or until lightly browned. Add the mushrooms and sauté over a high heat, stirring most of the time, until the mushrooms have absorbed all the oil in the pan.

Reduce the heat to low. When the juices have come out of the mushrooms, increase the heat again and sauté for 4–5 minutes, stirring most of the time, until the juices have almost evaporated. Add a squeeze of lemon juice and season to taste with salt and pepper. Stir in the parsley and cook for a further minute.

Transfer the sautéed mushrooms to a warmed serving dish and serve piping hot or warm. Accompany with chunks or slices of crusty bread for mopping up the garlic cooking juices.

Dips & Spreads

serves 6

225 g/8 oz cooked or drained
canned chickpeas

150 ml/5 fl oz tahini, well
stirred

150 ml/5 fl oz olive oil, plus
extra to serve

2 garlic cloves, coarsely
chopped

6 tbsp lemon juice

1 tbsp chopped fresh mint

salt and pepper

1 tsp paprika

pitta bread, warmed, to serve

hummus

Put the chickpeas, tahini, olive oil and 150 ml/5 fl oz water into the blender and process briefly. Add the garlic, lemon juice and mint and process until smooth.

Check the consistency of the hummus and, if it is too thick, add 1 tablespoon water and process again. Continue adding water, 1 tablespoon at a time, until the right consistency is achieved. Hummus should have a thick, coating consistency. Season with salt and pepper.

Spoon the hummus into a serving dish. Make a shallow hollow in the top and drizzle with 2–3 tablespoons olive oil. Dust with paprika and serve with warmed pitta bread.

serves 6

2 slices white bread, crusts removed

5 tbsp milk

225 g/8 oz smoked cod's roe

2 garlic cloves, coarsely chopped

150 ml/5 fl oz olive oil

2 tbsp lemon juice

2 tbsp natural Greek-style yogurt

pepper

black olives, to garnish

taramasalata

Tear the bread into pieces and place in a shallow bowl. Add the milk and set aside to soak. Meanwhile, using a sharp knife, scrape the cod's roe away from the outer skin.

Tip the bread and milk into a blender and process until smooth. Add the cod's roe and garlic and process again. With the motor running, gradually pour in the olive oil through the feeder tube. Process until smooth and the consistency of mayonnaise.

Add the lemon juice and yogurt and season with pepper. Process very briefly to mix, then scrape into a bowl. Cover with clingfilm and chill in the refrigerator until required. Garnish with black olives to serve.

serves 6

juice of 1 lime

3 avocados

2 garlic cloves, chopped

3 spring onions, chopped

2 fresh green chillies, chopped

2 tbsp olive oil

1 tbsp soured cream

salt

cayenne pepper, to garnish

tortilla chips, to serve

spicy guacamole

Put the lime juice into the blender. Halve the avocados and remove the stones. Scoop out the avocado flesh with a spoon straight into the blender.

Add the garlic, spring onions, chillies, olive oil and soured cream and season with salt. Process until smooth. Taste and adjust the seasoning with more salt or lime juice.

Spoon the guacamole into a serving dish. Dust lightly with cayenne pepper and serve with tortilla chips.

serves 6–8

2 large aubergines

2 red peppers

4 tbsp olive oil

2 garlic cloves, roughly chopped

grated rind and juice of 1/2 lemon

1 tbsp chopped fresh coriander

1/2–1 tsp paprika

salt and pepper

bread or toast, to serve

aubergine & pepper dip

Preheat the oven to 190°C/375°F/Gas Mark 5. Prick the skins of the aubergines and peppers all over with a fork and brush with about 1 tablespoon of the olive oil. Put on a baking tray and bake in the oven for 45 minutes, or until the skins are beginning to turn black, the flesh of the aubergine is very soft and the peppers are deflated.

When the vegetables are cooked, put them in a bowl and immediately cover tightly with a clean, damp tea towel. Alternatively, you can put the vegetables in a polythene bag. Leave them for about 15 minutes until they are cool enough to handle.

When the vegetables have cooled, cut the aubergines in half lengthways, carefully scoop out the flesh and discard the skin. Cut the aubergine flesh into large chunks. Remove and discard the stem, core and seeds from the peppers and cut the flesh into large pieces.

Heat the remaining olive oil in a large, heavy-based frying pan, add the aubergine flesh and pepper pieces and fry for 5 minutes. Add the garlic and fry for a further 30 seconds.

Turn all the contents of the frying pan on to kitchen paper to drain, then transfer to the bowl of a food processor. Add the lemon rind and juice, the chopped coriander, the paprika and salt and pepper to taste, and blend until a speckled purée is formed.

Turn the dip into a serving bowl accompanied with thick slices of bread or toast.

serves 4

3 large garlic cloves, finely chopped

2 egg yolks

225 ml/8 fl oz extra virgin olive oil

1 tbsp lemon juice

1 tbsp lime juice

1 tbsp Dijon mustard

1 tbsp chopped fresh tarragon

salt and pepper

aïoli

Ensure that all the ingredients are at room temperature. Place the garlic and egg yolks in a food processor and process until well blended. With the motor running, pour in the oil teaspoon by teaspoon through the feeder tube until the mixture starts to thicken, then pour in the remaining oil in a thin stream until a thick mayonnaise forms.

Add the lemon and lime juices, mustard and tarragon and season to taste with salt and pepper. Blend until smooth, then transfer to a non-metallic bowl.

Cover with clingfilm and refrigerate until required.

serves 4–6

200 g/7oz Greek feta cheese, crumbled

55 g/2 oz Greek yogurt

2 tbsp extra virgin olive oil

zest and juice of one small lemon

small bunch of fresh mint, chopped

small bunch of fresh flat-leaf parsley, chopped

1/2 red chilli, seeded and chopped

pepper to taste

warmed pitta bread and olives, to serve

herbed feta spread

Place the crumbled feta, yogurt and olive oil in a food processor and blend for 30 seconds until combined.

Scrape the mixture into a bowl and then add the lemon zest and juice, mint, parsley and chilli. Season to taste with pepper and mix well.

Leave in the refrigerator to chill for at least half an hour before serving.

Serve with warmed pitta bread and olives.

serves 4

100 g/3¹/₂ oz canned anchovy
fillets

350 g/12 oz black olives,
stoned and coarsely chopped

2 garlic cloves, coarsely
chopped

2 tbsp capers, drained and
rinsed

1 tbsp Dijon mustard

3 tbsp extra virgin olive oil

2 tbsp lemon juice

tapenade

Drain the anchovies, reserving the oil from the can. Coarsely
chop the fish and place in the blender. Add the reserved oil and
all the remaining ingredients. Process to a smooth purée. Stop
and scrape down the sides if necessary.

Transfer the tapenade to a dish, cover with clingfilm and chill in
the refrigerator until required. If you are not planning to use the
tapenade until the following day (or even the one after), cover
the surface with a layer of olive oil to prevent it from drying out.

serves 6

2 red peppers, halved and
deseeded

2 garlic cloves

1 tbsp extra virgin olive oil

1 tbsp lemon juice

25 g/1 oz fresh white
breadcrumbs

salt and pepper

red pepper dip

Place the pepper halves and garlic in a saucepan and add just
enough water to cover. Bring to the boil, then lower the heat,
cover and simmer gently for 10–15 minutes until softened and
tender. Drain and set aside to cool.

Coarsely chop the pepper halves and garlic and place in the
blender with the olive oil and lemon juice. Process to a smooth
purée.

Add the breadcrumbs and process briefly until just combined.
Season to taste with salt and pepper. Transfer to a serving bowl,
cover with clingfilm and chill in the refrigerator until required.

serves 6–8

250 g/9 oz whole beetroot

100 ml/3^1/$_2$ oz extra virgin olive oil

115 g/4 oz roasted hazelnuts

2 cloves garlic, peeled

115 g/4 oz fresh Parmesan cheese, freshly grated

salt and pepper

selection of crudités or bruschetta, to serve

beetroot & hazelnut pesto

Preheat the oven to 180°C/ 350°F/Gas Mark 5.

Sprinkle the beetroot with a little salt and pepper then drizzle with a small amount of the olive oil. Wrap the beetroot in foil and place in the oven. Cook for 1 hour. To test to see if the beetroot is cooked, poke with a small knife; the blade should go in with ease.

Remove the cooked beetroot from the oven and leave to cool. Once cool, peel away the skin and discard.

Place the hazelnuts and garlic in a food processor and process for 30 seconds.

Add the beetroot, salt and pepper and process again adding the olive oil a little at a time, through the feeder tube, until combined.

Pour the pesto into a bowl and mix in the Parmesan cheese.

Serve with crudités or spread on bruschetta.